Physician Alignment

Constructing Viable Roadmaps
for the Future

Physician Alignment

Constructing Viable Roadmaps for the Future

George Mayzell, MD, MBA, FACP
William R. Breen, Jr., MBA

Foreword by David Stern, MD, Executive Dean,
Vice Chancellor of Clinical Affairs,
UT College of Medicine

CRC Press
Taylor & Francis Group
Boca Raton London New York

CRC Press is an imprint of the
Taylor & Francis Group, an **informa** business

A PRODUCTIVITY PRESS BOOK

MIX
Paper from
responsible sources
FSC® C014174

CRC Press
Taylor & Francis Group
6000 Broken Sound Parkway NW, Suite 300
Boca Raton, FL 33487-2742

Printed in the United States of America on acid-free paper
Version Date: 20120615

International Standard Book Number: 978-1-4665-0476-9 (Hardback)

Library of Congress Cataloging-in-Publication Data

Mayzell, George.
    Physician alignment : constructing viable roadmaps for the future / George Mayzell, William R. Breen Jr.
        p. ; cm.
    Includes bibliographical references and index.
    ISBN 978-1-4665-0476-9 (hardcover : alk. paper)
    I. Breen, William R., 1962- II. Title.
    [DNLM: 1. Health Care Reform--organization & administration--United States.
    2. Delivery of Health Care, Integrated--organization & administration--United States.
    3. Models, Organizational--United States. 4. Physician Incentive Plans--organization & administration--United States. WA 540 AA1]

362.1--dc23

2012023898

Visit the Taylor & Francis Web site at
http://www.taylorandfrancis.com

and the CRC Press Web site at
http://www.crcpress.com

Contents

Foreword ix

Preface..xi

Acknowledgments xiii

About the Authors xv

1 Introduction: How We Got Here..1
   Historical Perspective..2
   Economic Imperatives..7
   Bibliography 11

2 Overview of the Future...13
   Introduction 13
   Physician and Hospital Trust 17
   Bibliography 19

3 Traditional Integration Models...21
   Medical Staff 21
   Medical Directorships...23
   Call Coverage 25
   Bibliography 27

4 Revenue of the Acronyms: Co-management, IPA, and
   PHO Integration Structure 29
   Introduction 29
   Clinical Co-management: Share the Gain 29
      Co-management Example 33
   The Independent Practitioners Association: How Exclusive Is the Club? 34
   The Physician Hospital Organization: Venus and Mars Form a Company.....35
   Bibliography 38

5 Physician Employment...**41**
    What Is Old Is New: Employment 41
    Employment Considerations.. 46
    Changing World: Making the Decision.....................................48
    Physician Employment Agreements 48
        From the Physician Side..48
        From the Hospital Side...50
        Physician View..51
        It Is All About Integration 56
    Foundation Model 56
    Physician Service Agreements 56
    Clinical Institutes 57
    Governance...57
    Physician Payment Models...59
    Appendix: Cultural Assessment Tool 62
    Bibliography 64

6 Clinical Integration...**67**
    What Is Clinical Integration?...69
    Bundled Payments 71
    Legal Limitations to Integration 73
    Information Technology 75
    Bibliography 77

**7 Accountable Care Organizations and the Patient-Centered
    Medical Home** **79**
    Introduction 79
    Accountable Care Organizations 80
    Patient-Centered Medical Home...86
        How Doctors Want to Be Paid for Providing a Medical Home.........92
    Bibliography 93

8 Assessing Your Current Alignment Strategy **97**

9 Examples of Systems Strategic Alignment Initiatives.........................**105**
    Methodist Le Bonheur Healthcare 105
    WILLIAM BREEN, JR.

    Geisinger Health System..106
    WILLIAM BREEN, JR.

    Piedmont Healthcare's Integration Strategy.............................109
    JAMES SAMS, MD

    Norton Healthcare System... 110
    GINGER FIGG

Summa Health System 112
NANCY A. MYERS, PHD

Hospital Physician Integration: Baylor Health Care System 115
DAVID J. BALLARD, MD and PAUL B. CONVERY, MD

Bibliography 117

10 Putting It All Together: Full Integration 119
Introduction 119
Blurring of Boundaries 120
Health versus Healthcare 120
Performance-Based System 121
Demographic and Environmental Factors 122
Legal Environment 123
Metrics and Transparency 123
Population Health 124
Physician Leadership 125
Patient Engagement 126
Transformation 127
Bibliography 129

Index 133

Foreword

Physicians are trained according to the time-honored principles that underlie the Oath of Hippocrates: curing the patient, when possible, and alleviating pain and suffering, while "doing no harm." Whether medical students were taught years ago, when I was trained, or today, in an interactive environment with problem-based learning and a vertically-integrated curriculum, the emphasis has been on maximizing one-on-one interactions between physician and patient. The development of a team concept for the physician is being increasingly recognized as a critical component of medical school training. The modern healthcare team is composed not only of physicians (primary care providers and specialists), but also of nurses, advanced practice nurses, allied health professionals, coordinators, social workers, and administrators. In the modern healthcare environment, the physician has evolved from the protective cocoon of the examining room to an integral participant in a system of care in which each piece is critical, but the whole is much greater than the sum of the component parts.

Administrators have traditionally had a somewhat stylized pattern of training which shapes their interaction with physicians and other personnel in the healthcare delivery system in a stereotyped manner. In some situations (for example, the classical hospital setting), the administrator has hegemony and the physician must comply with the orders. Alternatively, in the doctor's office, it is the physician who is the boss. The concept of an interactive team in which administrators, physicians, and others mentioned above are equal partners (and participants) in a system of care is not yet deeply ingrained in our training.

This book with chapters compiled by George Mayzell and Bill Breen attempts to bridge the gap between how we were trained and what we do today, versus the path forward into the future. For example...

- The chapter on clinical co-management, (physicians) independent practitioners associations and physician-hospital organizations emphasizes effective interactions between physicians and the health system. Although the business models are multiple and the legal ramifications complex, the underlying principle is that integration of physician skills with health system administration to achieve high quality outcomes, patient safety, and cost-effectiveness is a major undertaking; it requires many levels of involvement including evidence-based care pathways, chronic disease management protocols, etc.

■ The chapter on physician employment provides an abundance of practical information for doctors who may be considering such a transition. Refreshingly, the new models depart from the disappointing maxim, "what is in it for me?" The latter question asked by so many of our physician colleagues during this time of transition overlooks the central role of participating in a system of care which emphasizes a team-based approach to population health rather than one in which "piecework" is rewarded. The latter reflects a compensation system which has resulted in our currently nonsustainable healthcare spending in the USA. While compensation based on productivity currently has a central role in our reimbursement system, the importance of superior outcomes and quality of care, as well as addressing the "wellness" of a population, can be expected to take center stage shortly.

■ The chapter on clinical integration gets to the core of the matter as the acute care hospital is relegated to its appropriate position (one point or a few points) in the life cycle of care provided to an individual. The emphasis on preventive and rehabilitative care to preserve wellness and restore function, respectively, underscores the relative focus on long-term health in addition to provision of intermittent episodes of care in the hospital. The significance of transitions of care, as patients move from one level of care or provider to another, is similarly important as we consider the development of a system of care around a patient, rather than a patient simply interacting with a megapolis of medical services.

■ The final chapter on accountable care organizations and patient-centered medical homes moves from the conceptual to administrative embodiments of the principles of an integrated health system as we now know it. Of course, these names (and their respective acronyms) can be expected to be in perpetual transition. But, the concept of a team of dedicated healthcare and administrative professionals working in a patient-centered medical system is clearly preeminent.

As one who participates in medical school and health system administration, I recommend this volume for its emphasis on understanding and creating the health system of the future. We are entering a world in which the roles of healthcare professions and administrators will be blended into a structure melded around the patient, breaking down the silos instilled in us from our early training. Welcome to the contemporary and evolving world of healthcare!

David Stern, MD
Executive Dean, Vice Chancellor of Clinical Affairs
UT College of Medicine

Preface

We hope you will agree after reading Chapters 1 and 2 that our current path in healthcare is unsustainable. Clearly, there is an unlimited demand for limited healthcare resources. With our current aging population and technology advancements, we cannot possibly keep using our current broken and fragmented healthcare models. As healthcare leaders, we can play an active role at the local or regional level in strategies that increase value and maximize the use of healthcare resources. To do so will require new thinking.

After a long wait, the Supreme Court upheld the Patient Protection and Affordable Care Act (PPACA). Somewhat unexpectedly, the entire healthcare law was upheld in its entirety. It is difficult to predict what will occur in the future as we move toward a defining presidential election. Regardless, there has already been significant impact in many areas of healthcare, including within most healthcare organizations. The underlying premise that healthcare is just too expensive, with an increasing trend that is unsustainable, is not changed or altered by healthcare reform efforts, legislation, or the fact that the Supreme Court upheld the law. The increasing trends in the overall cost of healthcare are becoming unsustainable. There is simply not enough funding to maintain current healthcare spending without significant sacrifice of other critical needs.

This book is written for a broad group of audiences. It is meant to be an introductory primer on looking at healthcare delivery models and various types of integration. The audiences should include physician executives, physicians who are in practice looking at alignment, hospital administrators, and anyone who is involved in the healthcare delivery system. The articles covered in this book should affect everyone who is involved in healthcare.

The book starts setting the stage with Chapters 1 and 2 with an overview of the current trends in healthcare and why change is inevitable. We hope we make this argument compelling.

The next chapters focus on the different types of integration. While we do not go into any detail on some items, we start with the simplest types of integration (i.e., medical staff and medical directorships). We evolve quickly into full employment models with full integration. The last chapter tries to tie these together, bringing up all the other critically necessary factors for full integration, including patient engagement, information technology (IT) solutions, and others.

This book is not meant to be a guidebook or how-to-do-it book but as a means to set the stage to get people thinking about and understanding the various intricacies of integration. Each local market is different and subject to a different speed of change. It is often said that healthcare is always local, and we believe that is true. So, understanding the local market, politics, delivery systems, and legal environment becomes a critical factor in deciding what the right strategy for a particular system is.

In the long term, a full solution is much more complicated than simply physician and hospital integration. The entire healthcare system must be integrated in a meaningful way. This would include

- Full vertical and horizontal integration.
- Complete data sharing across the system. This includes clinical, cost data, and medical decision support.
- Complete transparency.
- Patient advocacy (one of the biggest challenges).
- Complete knowledge
- Transparency so patients understand the risks and benefits of any medical decision making.

Making this happen is a tall order and very complex, but we hope this book will help in your thinking process. This journey is going to be a bumpy road for the next several years but we hope it will end in a smooth landing after we get past the turbulence.

Acknowledgments

A special thank you to

Donna Abney
David Ballard, MD
Blayne Burns
Paul Convery, MD
Ginger Figg
Phyllis Gatlin
Dolores Leatherwood
Heather Mayzell
Nancy Myers, PhD
Ed Ralfalski
Jim Sams, MD
Gail Thurmond

About the Authors

George Mayzell, MD, MBA, FACP, FACHE, is a board-certified internist and geriatrician with over 10 years of patient care experience and over 19 years of administrative health industry experience.

Dr. Mayzell assumed the role of chief executive officer of Health Choice, LLC, in November 2010. Health Choice is one of the mid-South's leading physician hospital organizations, serving the needs of more than 518,000 health plan members through contracts with over 100 employers, insurance companies, and third-party administrators and 1,500 physicians through Metro Care Physicians. One of his recent projects is to create an accountable care partnership and an innovative system of patient-focused care.

Previously, Dr. Mayzell was senior vice president and chief patient care officer at Methodist Le Bonheur Healthcare. Methodist is a seven-hospital system with over 1,600 licensed beds in Memphis, Tennessee. He was responsible for patient care operations and oversight of regulatory readiness for the system. He also served as chief medical officer (CMO) for Methodist Germantown Hospital.

In addition to being a past faculty member at the University of Florida, Dr. Mayzell worked at Blue Cross Blue Shield of Florida, where he was directly involved with medical management activities, including disease management, utilization review, appeals and grievances, case management, pharmacy benefits, pay for performance, and Medicare risk.

Dr. Mayzell received his medical degree from New Jersey Medical and his MBA from Jacksonville University. He is the author of *Leveraging Lean in Healthcare* (CRC Press, 2011).

William R. (Bill) Breen Jr. has over 25 years experience in healthcare network leadership and relationship management. Bill worked at a large insurer from 1984 to 1991, building networks of physicians and hospitals to support managed care contracting. In 1991, he joined Methodist Healthcare in Memphis, Tennessee, to help lead a growing managed care network (Health Choice) that Methodist had built several years earlier. Bill rose to be the chief executive officer (CEO) of Health Choice in 1997 and assisted it through a reorganization as a full hospital/physician joint venture. During his tenure, the network grew to be the commercial market share leader in Memphis and developed numerous payer partnerships that benefitted the hospital system and over 1,200 physicians. He also led the development of services to aligned physicians that improved physician practice operations and loyalty to the health system. Bill now serves as the senior vice president of physician alignment for Methodist Le Bonheur Healthcare and is responsible for implementing and managing physician alignment activities for the system and remains as a board member of the physician-hospital organization (PHO). Bill has a bachelor's degree from the University of Louisville and a master's in business administration from the University of Memphis. He has achieved his fellowship in the American College of Healthcare Executives (ACHE) and is a certified medical practice executive in the Medical Group Management Association (MGMA).

Chapter 1

Introduction:
How We Got Here

There is broad agreement that the trajectory of the U.S. Healthcare System is unsustainable. I think that almost every provider group, every physician, recognizes that change is coming.

Elliott Fisher, director of Dartmouth
Center for Health Policy Research

Unquestionably, the U.S. healthcare system is in significant trouble. The U.S. healthcare expenditures surpassed $2.3 trillion in 2008, more than three times the $714 billion spent in 1990 and over eight times the $253 billion spent in 1980. The U.S. healthcare spending was about $7,681 per resident in 2008, accounting for 16.2% of the nation's gross domestic product ("U.S. Health Care Costs"). This is amongst the highest of any industrialized nation (Figure 1.1). In addition, the current system is increasingly inaccessible to many individuals, including the poor and middle class, with approximately 47 million Americans currently unable to get health insurance. Even with these astounding facts, the United States pays roughly twice as much per capita for healthcare as Canada, France, and the United Kingdom, yet experiences lower life expectancy and higher infant mortalities (Noah, 2007).

These facts suggest that the U.S. healthcare system is in significant trouble, and the solutions will be multifactorial. Alignment of provider payments will be critical for the future of healthcare in this country. Currently, physicians, hospitals, and other members of the healthcare system all have totally different and divergent incentives and are challenged in communicating patient information across different venues of care.

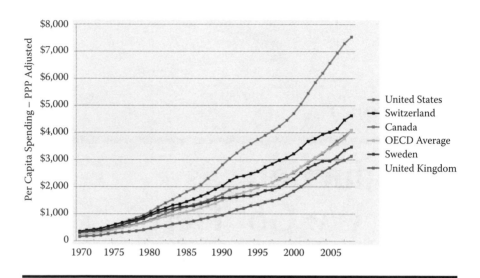

Figure 1.1 Growth in total health expenditure per capita, United States and selected countries, 1970–2008. Data from Australia and Japan are 2007 numbers. Figures for Belgium, Canada, Netherlands, Norway, and Switzerland are OECD estimates. Numbers are PPP adjusted. Break in series: CAN(1995); SWE(1993, 2001); SWI(1995); UK (1997). Numbers are PPP adjusted. Estimates for Canada and Switzerland in 2008. (The Kaiser Family Foundation, Kaiser fast facts, data source: Organisation for Economic Co-operation and Development (2010), "OECD Health Data", *OECD Health Statistics* (database). doi: 10.1787/data-00350-en Accessed on 14 February 2011).

The healthcare delivery system is extremely fragmented, particularly between hospitals and physicians. Currently, the physicians maintain the medical staff; the hospital administration controls the hospital. The payment structure and their alignment are not in sync with a patient-centric orientation.

Historical Perspective

We first take a quick look at the development of our healthcare system from a strategic level, looking at how physicians, hospitals, and other healthcare payment models have evolved over time and have put us in this predicament. To understand how we got here, it is helpful to go back and examine some of the history of healthcare delivery in this country (Figure 1.2).

Prior to the 1900s, hospitals were often small and focused on patients who were poor, old, or had chronic incurable diseases. The cost structure was less than $1.50 per patient per day. The patients were often in large wards and did a lot of the daily care themselves. Some of the patients would care for other patients; as a result, there was a "healing" social environment that surrounded this ward system.

1900s	1910s	1920s	1930s	1940s
American Medical Association (AMA) becomes a force; "organized medicine" is born.	American hospitals are on their way to becoming scientific institutions.		Social Security Act is passed.	Prepaid group healthcare is born.
	Reformers argue for health insurance.	Higher cost of medical care is a new and dramatic development.	Blue Cross begins offering private coverage for hospital patients.	During World War II, wage and price controls are placed.
Doctors are no longer expected to provide free services to hospital patients	Entry of the United States into the war in 1917 undermines healthcare insurance efforts.	General Motors signs a contract with Metropolitan Life to insure 180,000 workers.		Companies begin to offer health benefits.
		Penicillin is discovered.		

continued

Figure 1.2   Medical history since the 1900s. (From PBS, "Healthcare crisis: healthcare timeline." n.d. http://www.pbs.org/healthcarecrisis/history.htm)

1950s	1960s	1970s	1980s	1990s	2000s
National healthcare expenditures are 4.5% of GNP.	In the 1950s, the price of hospital care doubled.	Richard Nixon renames prepaid group healthcare plans as health maintenance organizations (HMOs).	Corporatization of healthcare begins.	Healthcare costs rise at double the rate of inflation.	Healthcare costs increase.
Private insurance for those who can afford it and welfare services for the poor exist.	Over 500 insurance companies are selling health insurance.	Healthcare costs are escalating rapidly.	Medicare shifts to payment by diagnosis (DRG).	There are 44 million Americans who have no health insurance.	Direct-to-consumer advertising exists.
Many more medications are available.	There is concern about a "doctor shortage."	The World Health Organization declares smallpox eradicated.	"Capitation" payments to doctors become common.	HIV/AIDS is rampant.	
	Lyndon Johnson signs Medicare and Medicaid into law.				

Figure 1.2 (continued)

Patients would help care for one another, and this in turn would help pay for their own hospital stay. Physicians did charity work on these wards. Full-time staff was often composed of hospital resident physicians. During this time, there were occasional strikes of physicians, which often resulted in the doctors being discharged. House staffs were dependent on the authority of the hospital owners or trustees. These hospital superintendents did not hesitate to reprimand or dismiss difficult doctors. For example, in the late 1890s a protest by the physician staff concerning living and working conditions resulted in dismissal of the entire staff. Can anyone imagine this happening in today's current model?

In the 1920s and into the 1930s, scientific treatments started to enter hospitals. Penicillin was discovered. There was, at this point, no healthcare coverage; however, hospitals did start to develop formal medical staffs. Hospitals were still very small and were more about shelter and caring for the poor than they were about providing medical care. Even though some treatments were developed (penicillin), they were not routinely available.

In the 1930s, the Great Depression began, and the Social Security Act was passed. It was at this time that Blue Cross started a prepaid insurance plan at the Baylor Hospital in Dallas, Texas. Everyone had the same premium structure, and this prepaid health plan was initially set up to cover only hospitalizations. Physician payments were still fully out of pocket.

From 1940 to 1960, prepaid healthcare started to increase. Penicillin began to be used, and the modern age of scientific medical care was in full swing.

World War II broke out during this time, causing wage and price controls to be put in place. This was a significant watershed moment in the history of healthcare. At this time, to attract or maintain the limited availability of good employees, companies started increasing benefits. Companies could no longer raise wages under price controls. Therefore, health insurance was now added as a benefit, and employer-sponsored healthcare was begun in earnest. This is how we got to where we are today, with most of our citizens covered under employer-sponsored health plans.

Blue Shield was started in 1946 to provide insurance on the physician side, whereas Blue Cross was only on the hospital side. Blue Cross and Blue Shield both were both created to make sure that the physicians and hospitals were fully paid. They typically paid the "usual-and-customary" amount (or 100%) of the billed charges. This was one of the original drivers of healthcare inflation. It was also at this time, after World War II, that the government got involved in providing healthcare as well.

Hospitals struggled to survive and maintain payments under the welfare and charitable care system. They were forced to attract and encourage private medical physicians to practice at their hospitals. Up to this point, hospitals were staffed by resident physicians only. Once private physicians were solicited to practice in hospital systems, the hospital had to develop a tiered system to attract wealthier patients. This required nicer facilities, amenities, and a separate ward system for charitable care. This created a hierarchy of care in each facility. It is at this point that hospitals started moving toward professional medical staffs, and the modern-day healthcare era began.

From 1950 to 1960, healthcare costs began to rise. In 1950, the healthcare cost in the United States was 4.5% of the gross national product (GNP). By 1960, hospital cost had doubled, and over 700 insurance companies were providing healthcare insurance to individuals. Specialist care was now starting to grow, and advancements in medicine were creating science-based hospitals and medical treatments. Prior to this, support and comfort were a large part of what physicians and healthcare providers offered.

In 1965, Medicare and Medicaid were brought into law. At this point, the expectation was that these would not be expensive programs. In 1950, the life expectancy of men was 66 years, and for women it was 72 years. However, with increasing life expectancy, Medicare became financially untenable.

In 1970 to the 1980s, healthcare costs continued to rise even faster. In the 1980s, the advent of managed care came into place as insurers and employers sought to pool purchasing power and, seeing usual-and-customary charges as the culprit, began to negotiate unit prices for healthcare services. With healthcare and the access to it becoming an increasing political football, Congress drafted the Health Information Portability Act of 1996 to assist in portability of employer-based overage.

Corporate management of healthcare systems was on its way. During the late 1980s, capitation had become a viable payment model in many cities. Under capitation, a fixed fee or a fee per member per month was paid to physicians or healthcare systems to take care of all of a patient's needs. This dramatically changed physicians' incentives.

In the 1990s, healthcare costs continued to rise, and in the early 2000s, Medicare and Medicaid accounted for 32% of the healthcare spending in the United States. Managed care was acting to control costs to some degree, and advertising directed to the customer was becoming rampant, especially around pharmaceuticals.

Spurred by divergent incentives and business models, by the late 1990s, hospitals had developed what is called a "workshop model." Hospitals and physicians were separate entities. Hospitals had their own administrative staff, often with a hierarchy in which each department was expected to be profitable, as was the entire hospital system. The hospital is paid by most payers under either a DRG (diagnosis related group, fixed payment by diagnosis) or per diem (daily rate) basis. Under this system, hospitals and physicians were reimbursed separately by Medicare A (hospital) and Medicare B (physician) payments. In 1983, the PPS (prospective payment system) took effect and put DRG payments in place for hospitals. Physicians cost reimbursement continued until 1992, when the RBRVS (Resource-Based Relative Value Scale) systems were put in place for physicians (still Fee-for-Service).

Hospitals were now focused on physicians and staff and less on patients. Hospitals had medical staffs to manage the quality of care and the physician environment and administrative staff to direct the business side of the hospital.

The payment structures and incentives had become different, and this is where the issues of the voluntary hospital staff began to play out.

We can see that with this convoluted history of healthcare and hospitals, the physicians and hospitals developed as separate entities and function separately. Future alignments both financially and structurally are extremely important for a successful healthcare system.

Economic Imperatives

The current structure of our healthcare system is preprogrammed to produce the rising cost that we currently experience. If you think about the hospital and physician relationships, the hospital currently acts as "a workshop" whereby the hospital runs all the ancillary facilities and the patient services at an expected profit. The physicians and medical staff are all volunteer medical staff; they voluntarily apply, submit to the bylaws of the hospital as directed by the medical staff, and then use the hospital to do their "service," which is treating patients. The billings for these services are totally separate; the hospital bills for the hospital side of the services, and the physicians bill for the physicians' side of the services. Often, the payment models are totally out of sync in that the hospital's goals for increasing payment are directly in conflict with the physician's goals of their payment. The patient gets lost in the middle. Quality outcomes and the value of services are not always obvious goals.

On the outpatient physicians' side, most practices are still cottage industries with only one or two physicians in a single practice (Figure 1.3). This is not an efficient model in that these are actually small business units run by an office manager and not linked with the other healthcare providers. While it is becoming more common for a practice to have electronic medical records (EMRs), which help physicians track the care and quality of each patient encounter, even so, these EMRs are not linked

Solo	37%
2 MDs	12%
3–5 MDs	28%
6–10 MDs	14%
11 or more MDs	9%

Figure 1.3 Practice size for office-based physicians. (From U.S. Department of Health and Human Services, Centers for Disease Control and Prevention, National Center for Health Statistics. Characteristics of office-based physicians and their practices: United States, 2005–2006, *Vital and Health Statistics* 13:1–34, April 2008. Available at http://www.cde.gov/nchs/data/series/sr_13/sr13_166.pdf.)

to each other and therefore function independently. In the future, it is expected that all of these EMRs will be connected through a health information exchange (HIE).

Even one's expectations from the banking industry are not obvious in the critical area of healthcare, where people's lives are at stake. Tests are duplicated, misread, read and not seen by the attending physician, lost in transit, and so on. A service as critical to the quality of life as healthcare would seem to demand a higher level of (electronic) systems.

A number of nonhospital and nonphysician entrepreneurships have entered into the hospital and physician relationship. These are other facilities such as those involving home health, durable medical equipment (DME), hospice, and others that may be owned by doctors, hospitals, or investors. These are profit-making entities that are often not easily coordinated for the transition of patient care.

Another issue with the current structure is that it is hospital-centric. The hospital is the source of capital for most investments, and much of healthcare revolves around the hospital and the hospital complex. Hospitals are clearly the most expensive place for healthcare, and it seems unlikely that hospitals will be the center of healthcare coordination and decision making in the future.

Currently, the system is extremely fragmented. Hospitals and physicians still account for the majority of cost increases according to the Centers for Medicare and Medicaid Services (CMS). For the period 2003 to 2008, hospitals accounted for 33% of the cost increases, while physicians' clinical services accounted for 34% of the cost increases; all other increases were in single digits.

In addition, the third-party payment structure leads to misaligned incentives in that patients do not pay for healthcare directly out of their pockets but instead pay for it through a copay or coinsurance (or through Medicare) (Figure 1.4). In this situation, the patient is only paying a small percentage of the actual cost of healthcare, so the patient is disconnected from the actual cost of healthcare. The other complicating pieces are legislation like EMTALA (Emergency Medical Treatment and Active Labor Act), which mandates that each hospital accept any patient from the emergency room and treat him or her. This makes the hospital responsible for what in most countries is considered a societal (government) responsibility. This cost must then be covered by insured patients and other paying patients. This is called *cost shifting.*

Also, there are opportunities in care transition. The system tends to be provider focused and not patient focused. The handoffs of clinical information from provider (or location of service) to provider are often incomplete or inaccurate. This accounts for duplication of care and occasionally poor outcomes. In addition, there are issues with end-of-life care and its extreme expense. The disconnection of patient financial responsibility and the high cost of care lead to excessive payments during this very expensive period of healthcare.

The payer mix and demographic changes in this country are significant and will continue to become more significant in the future (Figure 1.5). Clearly, the aging of the population or the "silver tsunami" with the baby boomers reaching older

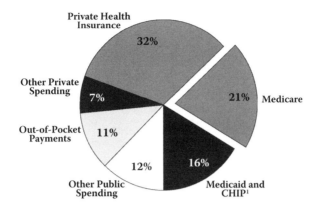

Total National Health Expenditures, 2010 = $2.6 Trillion

Figure 1.4 Projected national health expenditures in the United States, by source of payment, 2010. Includes Children's Health Insurance Program (CHIP) and Children's Health Insurance Program expansion (Title XIX).[1] Percentages do not sum to 100% due to rounding. (The Kaiser Family Foundation, Kaiser fast facts, from Centers for Medicare and Medicaid Services, Office of the Actuary, Updated National Health Expenditure Projections 2009–2019, January 2011.)

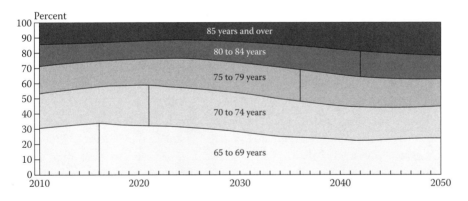

Figure 1.5 Distribution of the projected older population by age for the United States, 2010 to 2050. Note: Line indicates the year that each age group is the largest proportion of the older population. (From U.S. Census Bureau, 2008.)

ages is of critical concern. Another concern is that at age 65 today people live 50% longer on average than in 1940. By 2085, longevity of those aged 65 is projected to be 80% longer than in 1940 (data from the Social Security Administration Trustees Report, 2009).

The per capita healthcare spending by those 85 and above is seven times higher than that of those age 65 (data from Medicare and Medicaid Services National

- Indemnity
- Indemnify with Utilization Review
- PPOs (Preferred Provider Organization)
- HMOs (Health Maintenance Organization)
- Managed PPOs (Preferred Provider Organization)
- High Deductible Plans (CDHC-Consumer Directed Health Care)
- Integration with PFP (Pay for Performance)
- ACO (Accountable Care Organization)

Figure 1.6 Insurance trends.

Health Expenditures, 2008). In this scenario, the cost of healthcare from demographics alone is unsustainable. New technologies will add additional costs.

New healthcare legislation dealing with the uninsured could add anywhere from 35 to 45 million to the insured tax rolls, placing a huge demand on our healthcare system. These new patients will require additional primary care and other entry points into the system that will be difficult to create.

One current issue in the existing system is cost shifting, which occurs at the hospital. Patients who are uninsured are taken care of at the hospital using funds that come from commercial and Medicare payers. This, economists believe, is an unsustainable model. For example, a hospital in suburban New Jersey, the only one in the community, is demanding that health plans pay 15% more to compensate for Medicaid and Medicare payments that cost 4% to 5% less than the hospitals' own cost (Source: UHG Internal Contract Negotiation). These cost-shifting revenues will be difficult to maintain (Figure 1.6).

It is proven that increasing healthcare cost does not lead to increasing quality. A study by Fisher and Allen presented in a 2009 issue of the *New England Journal of Medicine* showed that the quality of care and health outcomes are often better in lower-spending regions. There have been no gains in survival in regions with greater spending growth. Thus, even though we are spending more money, we are not getting better healthcare.

The new reality of healthcare is that we have limited resources and will have to "do more with less." Of great concern currently are the rising national debt and mandatory entitlement programs such as Social Security, Medicare, Medicaid, and others. Just servicing the national debt is taking more and more of the federal budget. As the costs rise in healthcare entitlement programs, there will be less and less money for discretionary spending on things such as education, defense, and others. In fact, U.S. healthcare expenditures are projected to soar to more than one-third of the economy by 2040 (data from the CBO office, Long-Term Fiscal Outlook, June 2009). In the future, the share per capita consumption that is devoted to healthcare will rise from 24% in 2010 to 40% in 2030. It was 17% in 1990 (source data: Congressional Budget Office, Long-Term Budget Outlook).

The big challenge here is that rising cost does not equate to value and quality. To quote Warren Buffet, "Insurance is not the problem, the problem is incentives. We have payments for procedures, not for results" (Warren Buffet, chief executive officer, Berkshire Hathaway).

The driver of cost up to this point has not been one single factor, but multiple factors in different areas. (Ninety-five percent of every dollar cost increase is driven by healthcare providers, i.e., hospitals and physicians.) Sixty-seven percent of the increase of national healthcare spending is accounted for by rising prices as charged by the provider, not increased use of healthcare, but treatment volumes also are increasing, partly because of the rise of chronic diseases, obesity, and aging of the population. Thus, we have an unsustainable system that must adapt rapidly to future changes, leading to more efficient healthcare.

Bibliography

"American Hospitals." http://www.englisharticles.info/2011/07/08/american-hospitals/

CBO office, Long-Term Fiscal Outlook, June 2009. http://cbo.gov/sites/default/files/cbofiles/ftpdocs/102xx/doc10297/06-25-ltbo.pdf

Durable Medical Equipment (DME), http://www.cms.gov/Center/Provider-Type/Durable-Medical-Equipment-DME-Center.html?redirect=/center/dme.asp

Emergency Medical Treatment & Labor Act (EMTALA), http://www.cms.gov/Regulations-and-Guidance/Legislation/EMTALA/index.html

Fisher and Allen, *New England Journal of Medicine,* 2009, http://www.google.com/search?sourceid=navclient&ie=UTF-8&rlz=1T4ADFA_enUS443US444&q=New+England+Journal+of+Medicine%2c+2009%2c+Fisher+and+Allen#q=New+England+Journal+of+Medicine,+2009,+Fisher+and+Allen&hl=en&rlz=1T4ADFA_enUS443US444&prmd=imvns&ei=32UuUPWVO6KEygGC24C4Bw&start=10&sa=N&bav=on.2,or.r_gc.r_pw.r_qf.&fp=dc835c07362cbb1a&biw=1024&bih=657

Ginsburg, Paul B. Completion in health care: its evolution over the past decade. *Health Affairs,* 24(6): 1512–1522 (2005), http://www.healthaffairs.org/content/24/6/1512full

Global Library of Free Learning and Reading. American hospitals. July 8, 2011. http://www.englisharticles.info/2011/07/08/american-hospitals/.

"Health Reform and the Decline of Physician Private Practice." The Physicians Foundation, Merritt Hawkins, October 2010. http://www.physiciansfoundation.org/uploadedFiles/Health%20Reform%20and%20the%20Decline%20of%20Physician%20Private%20Practice.pdf

History of health care reform in the United States. http://en.wikipedia.org/wiki/History_of_health_care-reform_in_the_United_States, accessed January 22, 2012.

Medicare & Medicaid Services National Health Expenditures, 2008, http://www.cms.gov/Research-Statistics-Data-and-Systems/Statistics-Trends-and-Reports/NationalHealthExpendData/NationalHealthAccountsProjected.html

Noah, Timothy. A short history of health care. *Slate Magazine*, March 13, 2007. http://www.slate.com/id/2161736/.

Northern California Neurosurgery Medical Group. The history of health insurance in the United States. 2007. http://www.neurosurgical.com/medical_history_and_ethics/history/history_of_health_insurance.htm.

PBS. Healthcare crisis: healthcare timeline. http://www.pbs.org/healthcarecrisis/history.htm

Protzman, Charles, George Mayzell, and Joyce Kerpchar. *Leveraging Lean in Healthcare*. Boca Raton, FL: CRC Press, 2011.

Social Security Administration Trustees Report, 2009, http://www.ssa.gov/oact/tr/2009/tr09.pdf

Social Security Administration Trustees Report, 2009, http://www.ssa.gov/oact/tr/2009/index.html9

UHG Internal Contract Negotiation, http://www.unitedhealthgroup.com/hrm/UNH-Health-Care-Costs.pdf

U.S. Department of Health and Human Services, Centers for Disease Control and Prevention, National Center for Health Statistics. Characteristics of office-based physicians and their practices: United States, 2005–2006, *Vital and Health Statistics* 13:1–34, April 2008. Available at http://www.cde.gov/nchs/data/series/sr_13/sr13_166.pdf.

U.S. Health Care Costs. Centers for Medicare and Medicaid Services, Office of the Actuary National Health Statistics Group, National Health Care Expenditures, Data, January 2010. https://www.kaiserredu.org/Issue-Modules/US-Health-Care-Costs/Background-Brief.aspx

Chapter 2

Overview of the Future

Introduction

In the first chapter, we learned that the various components of healthcare evolved in very different ways, leading to dramatic disparity in financing mechanisms. Sustained financing of healthcare delivery in the future will demand a strong alignment between the parties providing healthcare and the payers financing it. These alignments (aligned incentives) must be cemented together to allow healthcare to become more efficient with better outcomes. The current financing system is broken, and the only way to get to a sustainable future is by removing waste and inefficiencies. We must take advantage of technology and provide even better care, using fewer resources. This is particularly true as the population ages and with growth of chronic diseases.

There are different methods of integration that can be achieved. They can range from contractual agreements and partnerships to employment models, as noted in Figure 2.1. Traditionally, we have had a voluntary model in which hospitals and physicians willingly agree to work together in a symbiotic relationship. Some of these loose integration strategies include medical directorships, call coverage agreements, small IPAs (independent practice associations), and MSOs (medical service organizations). This is what could be called level 1 integration.

Level 2 integration includes concepts such as physician-hospital organizations, joint ventures, gain sharing, clinical comanagement agreements, and physician service agreements (PSAs). In these models, there is alignment of payment, which is either bundled or shared in some form so that everyone is (from an economic standpoint) trying to minimize resource utilization. Quality incentives and measurable metrics are built into these programs. Hospitals and physicians must work together in these aligned incentives. This is only the beginning of integration opportunities.

Integration Model	Description
No financial integration	A physician has no financial ties to a hospital and is practicing independently.
Directorships and on-call payment	Physician leaders are more directly in the management and operations of a service line. Must be for services actually needed by the hospital and provided by the physician.
Joint ventures	Hospital and physicians partner to create a company as a provider of services.
Contractual agreement	Contractual agreements between a hospital and physician or physician group to provide a service on the hospital's behalf, including call coverage or professional services agreements. Co-management or service line management agreements offer opportunities to engage physicians directly in service line growth and quality improvement.
Leasing	Leases space, equipment, or staff.
Employment	Physicians are employed for medical services; salary is paid by a hospital, medical foundation, provider-based clinic, faculty practice plan, or a group practice.

Figure 2.1 Types of integration.

The third level of integration includes traditional employment models, foundation models, and hospital-owned clinic models. These models have the potential for full clinical integration with information sharing across all entities, including outcome measures. These models can also accept bundled payments so that any profit is shared in a fair and equitable fashion among the partners. This level gets us closer to full integration.

In all of these integration models, the providers will have new roles and responsibilities. There will be significant changes for many of the participants. In our current environment, the hospital is the center of healthcare, and much of healthcare, from leadership, management, and cost standpoints, starts with the hospital. The hospital's role should become ancillary in these new models; however, this is complicated by the fact that many hospitals are now purchasing physician practices. When payment is made based on outcomes and performance,

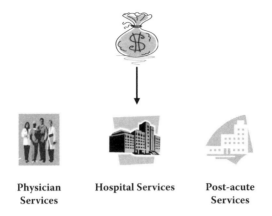

Physician Services   **Hospital Services**   **Post-acute Services**

Figure 2.2 Bundled payments diagram.

the hospital shifts from its traditional role of being a profit center to that of a cost center.

Currently, the majority of insured patients admitted to the hospital lead to a profit (or at least contribution margin) for the hospital since it is paid directly from a third party. Future models will prepay payments with lumped or bundled payments (Figure 2.2). Hospital treatment is the most expensive part of care, and proper incentives will lead to a reduction in this part of healthcare. In this situation, the hospital becomes a cost center where every patient admitted will cost additional money that might be used more efficiently in other settings. The hospital and providers will be rewarded for maintaining empty beds and being efficient about their use of the beds when medically necessary.

This new payment system will require strong physician leadership and a greater use of outpatient and preventive care (and wellness). In this model, there will be rewards for keeping patients out of the hospital and out of other expensive care venues. Decisions will have to be carefully balanced with both clinical and financial considerations. There will be a need for physician-driven leadership and physician engagement in the business side of medicine to handle this balance successfully.

Leading organizations through this transition will be a difficult task. Currently, the system is in transition, and the payment models are set up to pay based on volume of visits. There are no consequences to provide more care. There are also no consistent negative incentives for readmissions or not to perform expensive high-end testing for physicians. Leadership in the new paradigm will be required to build models that pay for performance and not just for clinical activity/volume. The critical challenge for any health system will be not to get too far in front of the payment curve. Focusing only on performance and quality and not on volume before the payment model changes could bankrupt a system. Leadership will be needed to balance the new and old models in this hybrid environment. This is reminiscent of the capitation days when practices struggled with having part of their practice capitated and part of their practice fee for service. This duality causes different styles of practice that are often not compatible.

One important point to remember is that in this current frenzy of hospitals buying physician practices is that ownership is not synonymous with integration. If a hospital buys a physician practice, it expects to control the physician referrals into their hospital for testing and for admissions. Physicians traditionally will refer where they feel patients get the best care and service. If the hospital services or employed providers do not meet these standards, particularly on the service side, physicians will hedge their bets and refer to their original referral patterns. This was true in the past days of employment (in the 1990s). Physicians, as employees, do not often respond as expected by hospital administrators.

Another concern is that resources must be removed from the system. When a physician refers to the hospital for testing and admissions, it can often be more expensive than other alternatives. In this case, integration will require a different payment model that rewards both the physician and the hospital not only for doing the right thing clinically but also doing it in the most cost-effective manner. The model should reward quality of care and the efficiency of care (Figure 2.3). This requires different cost structures at the hospitals' testing facilities as well as an effort to limit unnecessary admissions and to reallocate those resources to lower-cost alternatives. Ownership and employee relationships will not meet the standards of clinical integration and improved outcomes. Ownership alone does not create an efficient model of care. One can have clinical integration and efficient care with or without employment; therefore, employment does not automatically imply integration.

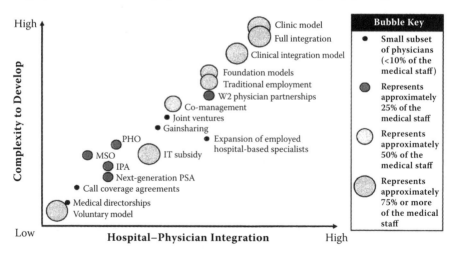

Figure 2.3   Integration versus complexity chart. (From Confidential & Proprietary © 2012 Sg2. Reprinted with permission.)

Physician and Hospital Trust

Trust levels between physicians and hospitals have never been particularly good. Even with the current relationships changing and slow alignment of incentives, there is still a lack of trust between the two groups. There is a lot to overcome. For example, in a Pricewaterhouse Coopers (PWC) survey (2011) it was indicated that 1 in 5 physicians do not trust hospitals, and 6 in 10 hospitals think it would be difficult to get health information from community physicians to provide more effective and efficient care.

The physician-hospital relationship has always been distrustful, but was particularly strained after hospitals bought (and then sold) hundreds of physicians' practices in the early 1990s. Hospitals tried to employ physicians and were, for the most part, unsuccessful. This further fractured an already-tenuous relationship with many physicians. As a result, many physicians sought better economies by opening competing entities to hospitals, such as outpatient surgery centers, outpatient imaging centers, and specialty hospitals. Single-specialty hospitals, such as those for orthopedics, cardiology, and others, diverted high-margin patients from the hospital and directly competed for services. During this time, hospital-physician joint ventures were created, which did help improve these working relationships but did not seem to increase trust.

Even though the trust relationship is still very fragile, nearly 71% of physicians surveyed by Pricewaterhouse Coopers already had aligned financially with hospitals through some model, whether employment, joint venture, or medical directorships; 58% of these respondents said they wanted to move to a closer relationship with the hospitals, and nearly one-fourth or 24% said they already worked primarily in a hospital practice setting. Even though the relationships are getting stronger and more aligned financially, there is still a strong element of mistrust and a lack of physician engagement.

Certain specialties are now almost completely aligned; an example is cardiology, which has two-thirds or approximately 63% of specialists aligned with hospitals. This occurred because of the significant Medicare cuts these practices have faced, particularly on the diagnostic and technical side of their practice incomes. The business models of many cardiology practices were upended by these changes.

When physicians were asked why they think hospitals wanted to align with them, 68% said that they believed that, first and foremost, hospitals are looking to consolidate market power to negotiate higher reimbursement rates with payers.

Sixty-four percent also believed hospitals want to improve patient outcomes, and 56% thought hospitals want to align with physicians to enhance coordination of care. It is clear that most physicians believed that hospitals and physicians will become more closely aligned over the next several years.

In today's model, hospitals and physicians are both rewarded for increasing volumes and treating sicker patients. Changing incentives will reward both sides for avoiding expensive inpatient facilities and treatments.

Even though financial and other pressures will drive hospitals and physicians closer together, it will take some time before the trust factor evolves. Physicians and administrators tend to think differently about things, and they are trained in very different ways. Physicians often have a difficult time grasping business concepts and views of administrators relating to balancing revenues, payments, profits, and patient care. Administrators often have a difficult time understanding the pressures of a medical practice, the decision-making model the physicians are trained in, and the time constraints on physicians in making and managing business decisions. It is hoped that, over time, both will become more comfortable and appreciative with understanding the important role they both play in a sustainable care model.

"Physicians are naive and do not realize that healthcare is expensive and that we need to have revenues, so that we can afford to pay for healthcare," said a savvy hospital administrator. On the other side of the table, physicians say that "administrators do not care about patients or quality; they only care about the bottom line." These are typical perceptions that physicians and hospital administrators have of each other.

It appears that physicians and hospitals are at extremes and have very different goals; however, both are committed to providing quality care and good outcomes in a cost-effective manner. This conflict arises because each group individually perceives that they are responsible for these objectives and that these objectives are mutually exclusive.

Physicians are taught through the educational process that discussion and dissent will not be taken as a professional insult or will be seen as personal criticism. It is even rewarded. In the administrative world, dissent by a physician is often taken personally. Also, in the decision-making process, an administrator will seek information from a number of parties, including physicians, and then reach a decision that meets organizational and patient care needs. Physicians make unilateral decisions without input since this is part of their training. They often see administrators as slow to make decisions and disrespectful of them in this process.

Conflict and strife between physicians and administrators can result in less-optimal outcomes. One of the more intriguing paradoxes is that physicians and administrators will resist changing this complex relationship status because it is easier to ignore the conflicts than to deal with them. The status quo contributes to their own identities, with each one feeling superior to the other.

The traditional role with the physician in control of the delivery of healthcare has been gradually eroding as corporations, employment models, clinical co-management arrangements, and other models become a part of the delivery of healthcare. This shift requires a change of attitude in both the physicians' and the administrators' traditional views. Only in a collaborative model can the healthcare delivery system meet efficiency and quality objectives.

Bibliography

A comparison of decision-making by physicians and administrators in healthcare settings, http://www.ncbi.nlm.nih.gov/pmc/articles/PMC1751052/

Bertko, John and Effros, Rachel. Analysis of bundled payment, *RAND Health Quarterly*, 1(3):15, 2011, http://www.rand.org/pubs/periodicals/health-quarterly/issues/v1/n3/15.html

Cross, D.A. Solving physician-hospital administration conflicts: a physician strategy for the 90s—Medial staff relations, http://www.ncbi.nlm.nih.gov/pubmed/10122612

Fiol, C. Marlena, and O'Connor, Edward J. Separately together: a new path to healthy hospital-physician relationships, at the Business School, University of Colorado Denver, February 18, 2010. http://business2.ucdenver.edu/Community/News/stories/10_0322.htm.

Matheson, David S., and Kissoon, Niranjan. A comparison of decision-making by physicians and administrators in healthcare settings. *Critical Care*, 10:163 (2006). http://www.ncbi.nlm.nih.gov/pmc/articles/PMC1751052/.

McGuireWoods and Sg2 Staff, Accelerating Hospital-Physician Collaboration, Sg2 Edge Web Seminar, November 12, 2008 http://members.sg2.com/content-detail-events-previous/?contentid=2275482

Medical Group Management Association (MGMA). Report: physicians, hospitals seek closer relationships, but trust remains an issue. http://blog.mgma.com/blog/bid/65002/Report-Physicians-hospitals-seek-closer-relationships.

Meyer, Harris. Quality models. *Managed Healthcare Executive.* November 1, 2009. http://managedhealthcareexecutive.modernmedicine.com/mhe/article/articleDetail.jsp?id=638750&sk-&d.

Pricewaterhouse Coopers 2011, From courtship to marriage: A Two part series on physician-hospital alignment. Part I: Why health reform is driving physicians and hospitals closer together, Part II: How physicians and hospitals are creating sustainable relationships. http://www.pwc.com/us/en/health-industries/publications/from-courtship-to-marriage-series.jhtml

Umansky, Ben. Succeeding Under Bundled Payments. http://www.advisory.com/~/media/Advisory-com/Research/HCAB/Research-Study/2010/Succeeding-Under-Bundled-Payments/Succeeding-Under-Bundled-Payments-HCAB.pdf

Chapter 3

Traditional Integration Models

Medical Staff

Traditional medical staff models date back to the initial quality improvement efforts of physician leaders as early as the 1900s. The American College of Surgeons was the first to formalize an approach to this in 1919, establishing voluntary standards that defined what a medical staff should do for approved hospitals.

This concept evolved and matured and, in 1951, spurred the creation of the Joint Commission on Accreditation of Healthcare Organizations (JCAHO). There were several centers of authority at hospitals during this time, including the governing board, physicians, and executive management. This was a loosely integrated model, and it was ultimately JCAHO that required accredited hospitals to have organized medical staffs whose main function was to oversee clinical practice and quality of care provided by the physicians who had staff privileges. This function still exists in the medical staff bylaws today.

In early legal cases, including *Darling v. Charleston Memorial Hospital* and *Johnson v. Misericordia Hospital*, courts clearly established the linkages and accountability of the hospital for the actions of its medical staff. These responsibilities, through the concept of vicarious liability, exist today whether physicians are employed or volunteer medical staff. Effective performance of an organized medical staff includes such things as credentialing, delineation of privileges, and responsibility for the quality of care. In exchange for these activities, the hospital provides a safe environment with appropriate professional and technical staff as well as proper equipment to perform appropriate testing and procedures.

More recently, medical staff responsibilities have evolved to include peer review and validation of physician credentials, delineation of privileging (specific duties the physician may perform as part of hospital care), quality review, and continuing medical education. They also participate in the hospital accreditation process.

This new collaborative medical staff relationship is a move in the right direction; however, there are still many misaligned incentives between the hospital and physicians. Some of this new work requires increasing the time dedicated to medical staff activities and has evolved to paid positions for some of these physicians' roles, which were traditionally voluntary.

Hospitals currently maintain significant support staff to help with medical staff functions and to help with the administrative aspects of managing the medical staff process. The process of selecting leaders was typically an appointed role from the hospital, although more and more leadership roles are evolving into elected positions. The elections and the willingness of the physician leaders to handle these roles voluntarily are becoming more controversial.

One of the responses to the new challenges of medical staff management is lengthening the term of each role with a clear succession plan so future leaders have time to learn in this increasingly complex environment. These are incredibly demanding positions that require skills that many physicians do not currently have as well as demanding a significant amount of their time. This sometimes leads to having the wrong medical leaders involved in the medical staff process. Current issues with medical staff management include the continuing power struggle between primary care and specialists. In addition, another emerging group of physicians, the hospital-based physicians, seem to be taking an increasing role in medical staff management. Many of the medical staff members feel uncomfortable with these physicians in these roles since they have a financially aligned position with the hospital. Many times, they have exclusive contracts with the hospital. Also, primary care physicians are often not participants in the medical staff process in an active way. Hospital processes are often specialty driven. Leaders are often specialists because of the financial advantages of specialty care or the time commitments required. This may create challenges in getting the right representation into the right positions. Leaders must be engaged in serving the entire medical staff, not their personal or group needs. This is a difficult situation for many medical staff entities to resolve.

The organized medical staff has traditionally been a weak forum for hospital physician integration. Leadership has not always been as strong as it should be and has not always been seen to consistently represent physicians. There was a time when rank-and-file physicians could not attend official hospital meetings or certain committees of the organized medical staff. This led to challenges in communication. One can see from the evolution of the formal medical staff that it has been a constant challenge and not an ideal way to integrate with a hospital system. Better ways are emerging with improved alignment both financially and philosophically.

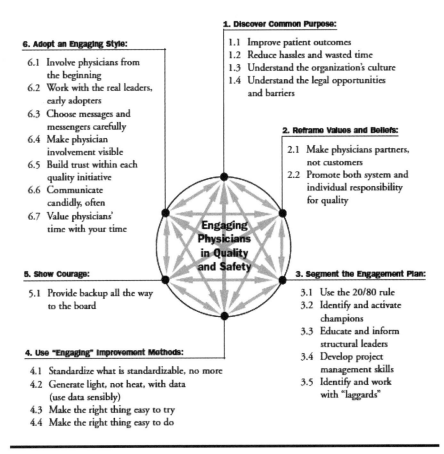

6. Adopt an Engaging Style:

6.1 Involve physicians from the beginning
6.2 Work with the real leaders, early adopters
6.3 Choose messages and messengers carefully
6.4 Make physician involvement visible
6.5 Build trust within each quality initiative
6.6 Communicate candidly, often
6.7 Value physicians' time with your time

5. Show Courage:

5.1 Provide backup all the way to the board

4. Use "Engaging" Improvement Methods:

4.1 Standardize what is standardizable, no more
4.2 Generate light, not heat, with data (use data sensibly)
4.3 Make the right thing easy to try
4.4 Make the right thing easy to do

1. Discover Common Purpose:

1.1 Improve patient outcomes
1.2 Reduce hassles and wasted time
1.3 Understand the organization's culture
1.4 Understand the legal opportunities and barriers

2. Reframe Values and Beliefs:

2.1 Make physicians partners, not customers
2.2 Promote both system and individual responsibility for quality

3. Segment the Engagement Plan:

3.1 Use the 20/80 rule
3.2 Identify and activate champions
3.3 Educate and inform structural leaders
3.4 Develop project management skills
3.5 Identify and work with "laggards"

Engaging Physicians in Quality and Safety

Figure 3.1 IHI framework for engaging physicians in quality and safety. (From Reinersten, James L., Alice G. Gosfield, William Rupp, and John W. Whittington. *Engaging Physicians in a Shared Quality Agenda.* IHI Innovation Series white paper. Cambridge, MA: Institute for Healthcare Improvement; 2007. Available at http://www.IHI.org. Reprinted with permission.)

Medical Directorships

One form of hospital and physician integration is the hospital employment of medical directors for specific services or service lines. This is an easy, cost-effective way to start the process of integrating physicians into the quality and service improvement initiatives of a hospital (Figure 3.1). It should be noted that recently both the Centers for Medicare and Medicaid Services (CMS) and the Office of the Inspector General (OIG) are starting to look at these agreements more carefully.

In this arrangement, the hospital retains the physician to provide guidance on clinical operations, patient services, or patient care activities. In an academic center, this can also be a paid position as a department head or department chair.

These physicians' input must add real value to the system, and the positions cannot simply be created to encourage referrals or provide additional compensation to physicians. There must be clear definition of expectations and responsibilities, and the compensation must be carefully matched with the degree of effort, time, and responsibility that the physician is undertaking. Agreements must be carefully constructed to include

- The medical director's responsibilities and obligations
- The number of hours per week that will be necessary
- The compensation to be paid (usually on an hourly basis)
- The term of the agreement and termination language (must be longer than 1 year)
- The specific time commitment for the physician and details regarding how the physician will document his or her activity

There are several laws that have an impact on these arrangements, including the Stark Law, the anti-kickback statute, and the Internal Revenue Code Section 501(c)(3). It is important to obtain legal advice as well as other professional advice prior to constructing one of these agreements. There are both monetary and other penalties if these agreements are not proven to be real "value added." Recently, CMS announced that it will issue Disclosure of Financial Relationship Reports (DFRRs) to selected hospitals. This is a way for CMS to collect information on these agreements and ensure greater government scrutiny.

Clear guidelines help limit exposure with careful documentation of the service that is rendered, with components such as a written contract with written documentation. There should be an actual contract longer than a year carefully documenting the services that will be provided.

- These services must be legitimate. The medical director should perform services that really are value added to the hospital and can be easily verified and justified.
- Daily logs should be kept, carefully documenting the amount of time involved, what was done, and what the value was for this service.
- The compensation should be "fair market value" (FMV) based on hourly fees.
- The fee should be constructed based on what the physician would earn if he were performing nonclinical care. The physician should be compensated based on what a similar person with similar skills would be paid (i.e., on an hourly basis, usually in the neighborhood of $150 to $250 per hour).
- This should be carefully monitored on an ongoing basis and should be well documented.
- The service of these individuals must be reviewed on a yearly basis with appropriate metrics to measure success and the benefit. Factors may have changed, and the relationship should be reevaluated to reflect these changes.

Many different items can be placed under a medical directorship, including the quality initiatives of the hospital, including CMS metrics and others. Medical directors may review outcomes or care processes. They may be involved in developing policies and procedures or be reimbursed for attending meetings where they provide clinical input.

Job functions usually take between 3 or 4 hours a week, although it is highly dependent on the role that the hospital and physician agree on.

The medical directorship responsibilities are a great way to help integrate a physician into the business of the hospital. They are also a great way for hospitals to understand their physician leaders better. At a time when physicians do not often receive business or leadership guidance, this can also be important training for the physician to successfully ensure more critical integration opportunities.

Call Coverage

When you ask a seasoned hospital administrator about call coverage, you are likely to get a roll of the eyes or a groan. It used to be the case that for the "privilege" of having hospital privileges, physicians would graciously accept the burden of caring for unassigned patients who presented in the emergency department, but times have changed.

Between 2006 and 2008, the median expenditures for on-call physician compensation grew by 88% in trauma centers in the United States. In nontrauma centers between 2007 to 2008, this increase was 118% in just 1 year. In fact, as Figure 3.2 indicates, this is an increasing problem for hospitals. The trend over the past decade has been toward physicians receiving compensation in exchange for the burden of being on call. For a multihospital system, this can be a slippery slope. Once the door is opened, it is difficult to shut. Whether it is a single hospital or a multihospital system, opening the door to one specialty call compensation invites similar demands from others. Those hospitals that have been successful in managing call coverage payments have set standards and implemented approval processes that ensure a more strategic mindset and consistent process behind negotiations with physicians. The implementation of the Emergency Medical Treatment and Active Labor Act (EMTALA) and subsequent increased enforcement of such regulations has created an environment with far more scrutiny of emergency department treatment and internal and external handoffs among physicians.

The reasons for the growth of call coverage payments are numerous. Many geographic areas face a shortage of physicians. In addition, the annual reimbursement adjustments to physicians no longer cover cost increases in many instances. Add to that a potential eroding payer mix and you can see why the more vulnerable hospitals with poorer payer mixes were the first to fall victim to these financial demands. Even physician demographics are driving the trend. Studies have shown that the younger physician is different from the older physician. The difference

Appendix A: California Hospital Association / The Performance Alliance
On-Call Survey Summary

TABLE 1. SCOPE OF PROBLEM	Serious Problem	Somewhat of a Problem	Not a Problem	
At your hospital, is the lack of an on-call physician coverage for the ED a problem?	12%	55%	33%	Surveys sent: 330 Responses: 110 Response rate: 33%

TABLE 2. CHANGE IN CALL DIFFICULTY	Has Become More Difficult	Has Become Less Difficult	Has Not Changed	Has Not Been a Problem in Our Organization	Not Sure/ No Opinion
Over the past five years, has the difficulty of ensuring adequate ED specialty coverage changed in your hospital?	51%	12%	25%	11%	1%

TABLE 3. ON-CALL STRATEGIES	Currently Doing	Implementing/ Considering	Stopped
Stipends	81%	1%	1%
ED throughput task force	75%	11%	4%
ED fast-track program	65%	8%	8%
Rapid Medical Exam (RMC©) or similar	50%	10%	4%
Mandatory call	47%	1%	9%
Exclusive contracts with specialists	40%	1%	3%
ED hospitalist program(s)	39%	11%	1%
Telemedicine or robotics	34%	18%	6%
Regional call arrangements	28%	9%	1%
Mix of stipends and guarantees	21%	5%	5%
ED observation unit	20%	15%	5%
PAs/NPs as first responders	19%	3%	2%
Contracting with another hospital	18%	2%	2%
Community call	12%	5%	1%
Third-party administered compensation program	11%	6%	0%
Specialty IPA for ED call coverage	9%	2%	0%
Deferred compensation program	5%	2%	1%
Non-economic incentives	3%	2%	2%

Figure 3.2 California Hospital Association: the Performance Alliance on-call survey summary. (Reprinted with permission from the California HealthCare Foundation 2012.)

is reflected in how these younger individuals think of work and the profession. Younger doctors place a greater value on free time and work/life balance. Asking a doctor to take the responsibility for unassigned care, make a trip to the hospital, and disrupt personal life without compensation now seems naïve.

As call relationships have evolved, so have the legal issues surrounding them. Today's hospital has to be vigilant about structuring such arrangements to reflect FMV for the physician's time. According to the Medical Group Management Association (MGMA) studies, the vast majority (over 97%) of arrangements struck between U.S. hospitals and on-call physicians involve a daily or hourly compensation methodology. Determining the FMV is usually a function of either surveys (MGMA and Sullivan Cotter being the most widely used) or prevalent locum tenens rates.

Although the hourly or daily rate methodology is far more common, other compensation methods are also used, including payment only for excess calls. In this method, call pay begins when and if the physician must take calls more than a fixed number of occurrences in a time period. If a medical staff is large enough and the call is split evenly, it is possible that the threshold is reached infrequently.

Given the demographic shifts we are facing in physician supply, payer mix changes, and reimbursement pressures, it is likely that private, nonemployed physicians will continue to demand pay for call coverage. More intense scrutiny is likely to mean that such arrangements will be legally tested. A hospital compliance program must ensure that each arrangement meets the standard of FMV. As employment of physicians increases, this could have a significant impact on how call coverage is compensated. Most facilities and physicians will act in their best interest, and when the cost to provide coverage reaches an inflection point, hospital employment of physicians will be used as a solution instead of compensating private physicians.

While compensating for on-call coverage creates an obligation between the physicians and the hospital, it does not necessarily create much in the way of alignment. It may be a sign of the times, but it can exacerbate an uneven reimbursement playing field between the hospital and the medical staff.

Bibliography

Addy, Jill. What are the latest trends in call coverage, sg2, March 12, 2008, http://members. sg2.com/content-detail-standard/?ContentID=1963307

AMDA, Medical director roles and responsibilities, March 2006. http://www.amda.com/ about/roles.cfm/

Call Coverage Agreements: Benefits and Challenges, Sg2, 2008, www.sg2.com, http://members. sg2.com/content-detail-standard/?ContentID=2263538, sg Intelligence, Sept. 10, 2008

Gosfield, Alice G. Rethinking the role of the medical staff in the New Quality Era, www.gosfield. com, 2005, http://www.google.com/url?sa=t&rct=j&q=rethinking%20the%20role%20 of%20the%20medical%20staff%20in%20the%20new%20quality%20era&source=we b&cd=1&sqi=2&ved=0CEUQFjAA&url=http%3A%2F%2Fgosfield.com%2FPPT%2 FVirtuaRethinking%2520The%2520MSRole.ppt&ei=h08pUPzLD9S1yQHazYDYCQ &usg=AFQjCNEF9NNZJY79zff39433rXvfXSzqzQ

Gosfield, Alice G. "AGG latest issues in the industry", www.gosfield.com, 2010, http://www.gosfield.com/newissues.htm

Hebron, Allison, Medical directorships: benefits and challenges, Sg2, 2008, www.sg2.com http://members.sg2.com/content-detail-standard/?ContentID=7766254624997622361

Hershey, Nathan. Documenting roles and responsibilities—Hospital Medical Director, *Physician Executive*, July–August 1990, http://www.highbeam.com/doc/1G1-9366233.html

Medical directorships: Increased OIG scrutiny highlights importance of structuring compliant agreements, www.governanceinstitute.com, December 2007, http://www.sillscummis.com/newsroom/publications/medical-directorships-increased-oig-scrutiny-highlights-importance-of-structuring-compliant-agreements.aspx

MGMA (Medical Group Management Association), Highlights of MGMA's 2011 Physician Compensation survey, http://mgma.com/blog/Highlights-of-MGMAs-2011-Physician-Compensation-survey/

Purtell, Dennis J. Medical staff in need of change, *Physician Executive*, January-February 2002, http://www.whdlaw.com/Publications/Purtell.pdf

Reinersten, James L., Alice G. Gosfield, William Rupp, and John W. Whittington. *Engaging Physicians in a Shared Quality Agenda*. Innovation Series white paper. Cambridge, MA: Institute for Healthcare Improvement, 2007.

Thompson, Richard E. Re-forming the traditional organization medical staff, *Physician Executive*, April 1995, http://www.ncbi.nlm.nih.gov/pubmed/10161193

Tocknell, Margaret D. Medical director duties, compensation vary widely, MGMA, May 5, 2011, HealthLeaders Media, www.mgma.com, http://www.healthleadersmedia.com/page-2/FIN-265731/MGMA-Medical-Director-Duties-Compensation-Vary-Widely##

Chapter 4

Revenue of the Acronyms: Co-management, IPA, and PHO Integration Structure

Introduction

Those of us who are blessed (or cursed) to work on the administrative side of health-care have become all too familiar with the trendiness of ideas and the plethora of acronyms that represent them. Faced with complex multiword concepts, any healthcare thinker or leader can turn that concept into an acronym. These acronyms serve a purpose as they make communication more efficient. This chapter discusses these acronyms, old and new, as well as recycled ones that are coming back into vogue.

Clinical Co-management: Share the Gain

In the ever-changing healthcare landscape, clinical co-management may be just what the doctor ordered. Healthcare, by its very nature, is constantly evolving and taking advantage of new developments and discoveries. This innate climate of innovation in healthcare is fostered through the meticulous reinvention efforts of the healthcare providers and administrators. Clinical co-management falls squarely into the business innovation category. Clinical co-management is an attempt to maximize the alignment of physicians and hospitals while producing a higher quality of care for patients (Figure 4.1).

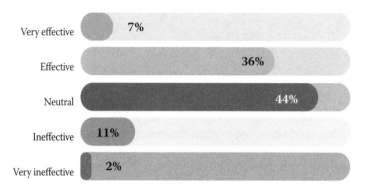

Figure 4.1 How effective are co-management models for service lines? (From HealthLeaders Media Industry Survey 2011, combined results from leadership, finance, physician, nurse, and quality leaders reports.

Clinical co-management shares the gain when it comes to alignment. The "holy grail" is a well-designed, legal, and properly incentivized program that is likely to produce a win-win outcome for all parties. Now that we have identified the goals, we can also admit that it often appears that these goals are mutually exclusive. There are only a few well-prescribed ways to align incentives if the issue of legality is a strategic prerequisite. The alignment and creation of incentives whereby facility savings are shared directly with physicians based on savings is not legal in the United States. Stark and other statutes whose goals were to preserve the quality of care by ensuring no direct financial benefit by a physician based on his or her clinical judgment prohibit sharing. Whether you view these laws as safety nets or a form of government intrusion, they are a reality. They certainly guarantee full employment for healthcare consultants and attorneys. But, in all fairness, they are not a total impediment to alignment. Clinical co-management is a concept growing in use and popularity in the healthcare community and operates inside the regulatory boundaries (Figure 4.2).

Clinical co-management is a new alignment relationship whereby physicians and a facility collaboratively co-manage a service line or clinical department. The potential outcome of this relationship is valued independently by an outside third party prior to implementation, and dollars are shared among participating physicians. The amount of money shared is based on a formula agreed on beforehand. In essence, funds flow for the achievement of predetermined improvements in efficiency, cost, and satisfaction. Usually, fees are shared on a fixed basis with MDs paid hourly for their work and on an incentive basis on agreed-on metrics. It is critical for reimbursement to be based on performance, and goals cannot be volume-based metrics.

The legal structure of a clinical co-management relationship often involves creating a new entity, a management company that can either be a wholly

	Benefits	*Challenges*
Hospital	Provide opportunities to align more closely with a group of physicians	Broad participation of the physician group is required.
	Directly engage physicians in the management of the service line	Careful documentation of physician time and ongoing involvement of legal counsel in monitoring the agreement are necessary.
	May provide opportunities for the cost savings and other efficiencies	Payments to physicians must be fair market value.
Physicians	Allow physicians greater sense of control over the service line	Compensation and return-on-investment possibilities for physicians are limited.
	Allow physicians to maintain independent practice	Physicians may inherit historic service line challenges, such as difficulty securing call coverage.

Figure 4.2 Sg2 benefits and challenges. (From Confidential & Proprietary © 2012 Sg2. Reprinted with permission.)

physician-owned entity or a joint venture with a hospital. The dollars shared by the hospital are distributed through the management company. Arrangements of this kind must achieve a certain size, scope, or relevance to justify the time commitment for the participants in managing the service line. In general, dollars at risk for payment under such a management fee can be from 1.5% to 3% of net revenue for the service line. Physicians often want to maintain either total or majority ownership of the management entity so that more dollars can pass to the MDs for providing the work. The dollar value placed on the achievement of the goals must be determined by an outside third party before the arrangement goes live. In addition, an attestation that the relationship meets fair market value (FMV) is usually required as well. One of the challenges of a successful co-management agreement is that as each of the quality metrics is achieved, the bar must again be raised for the subsequent year. This becomes self-limiting as the metrics become more and more challenging to achieve. Many feel that co-management is a progressive step toward more aligned models, such as employment. Co-management is a perfect construct to handle bundled payments that most believe are eminent.

In reviewing this alignment option, it is important to ask whether you possess the raw material for such a deal to make sense. The service line, whether it be

Co-management Structure

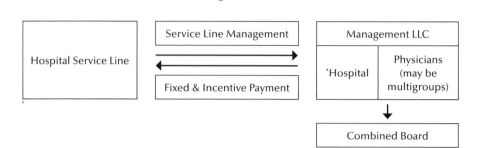

* Hospital may or may not be an LLC partner.

Figure 4.3   Co-management structure.

neurology, orthopedics, or others, must have a generally cohesive medical staff. There must be room for improvement in clinical efficiency and satisfaction metrics from the start. In addition, you must establish a relationship with a consulting and legal team that can assist you in reviewing all components of the arrangement. It very well could be that you do not have the right environment or it is not the right time to successfully structure clinical co-management. Co-management can work extremely well when you have multiple subspecialty providers practicing in different groups (Figure 4.3). They can then be aligned without any type of employment or clinical integration through a co-management structure.

Physician contracts can also be structured directly with the hospital for co-management services. This scenario is referred to as a *direct contract.* In other instances, a joint venture is created, with ownership split between the physicians and the hospital. The areas to be managed and where improvements exist will need to be vetted in the initial creation of these agreements. The terms of these agreements are typically from 1 to 3 years, with most renewable by mutual consent.

Much of the compensation is typically fixed, with the remainder based on metrics that can vary from one agreement to the next. The schedule of metrics may include operational process improvements, quality indicators, and satisfaction measures. A few examples are as follows:

- Creating a specific service line
- Physician staffing, patient scheduling
- Operational oversight
- Development of business plans and budgets
- Emergency room coverage

• Service line development
• Medical director services
• Community relations and education
• Patient, physician, and staff satisfaction
• Clinical protocols and performance standards
• Staff scheduling and supervision
• Work flow process changes
• Credentialing processes
• Materials management
• Case management
• Medical staff-related activities and committees

Figure 4.4 Co-management services. (From Ken E. Mack, FACHE, president, Ken Mack and Associates. With permission.)

The benefit of the co-management agreements can be significant for all of the involved parties (Figure 4.4). The hospitals may realize material savings and increased efficiencies within the system, while the physicians will be compensated for their contributions and feel a stronger sense of belonging to the hospital system. Physician participation in operational decisions at the hospital can be extremely advantageous for the hospital. Physicians who want to have a seat at the table and hospitals that recognize the value of the physician at the table can be a powerful alignment formula in today's healthcare landscape. The accord may also serve as a stepping-stone on the path to physician employment. The opportunity cost of not considering a co-management agreement may be significant to healthcare systems looking to reduce costs and increase quality and efficiency.

Co-management Example

One of the major examples of co-management is in the area of orthopedics. Orthopedics is a growing field, particularly with inpatient necessity, and the increasing volume of joint replacements. Aging and demographics are contributing to the hospitalization trends. To that end, it can be important to align orthopedic surgeons with hospitals, which creates a great opportunity for co-management.

These are often created as separate limited liability companies (LLCs), sometimes with the hospital as a partner, sometimes without. These LLCs can also include multiple different orthopedic groups, which then decide how the service line should be managed in concert with the hospital. Some key metrics in the area would include

- Risk-adjusted length of stay
- Unplanned transfers to the intensive care unit (ICU)
- Venous thromboembolism prophylaxis rates
- Hospital-acquired and catheter-acquired infections
- Patient satisfaction and provider satisfaction
- Readmissions
- Multiple financial metrics

There are also many quality metrics that could be measured, including complication rates of procedures (including postoperative complications), bed turnover, and discharge process metrics. Patient safety should also be included in this, such as post-operative glycemic control.

The Independent Practitioners Association: How Exclusive Is the Club?

Another potential alignment strategy for a hospital or healthcare system is to assist members of the medical staff in the formation of a physicians' independent practitioners association (IPA). Many IPAs were created in the 1980s and 1990s as a method to organize for managed care contract negotiations and capitation. Prior to Department of Justice (DOJ) rules implemented in the early 1990s, IPAs routinely negotiated price and payment terms with payers on behalf of their members. The DOJ ruled this behavior anticompetitive and forced IPAs to operate differently in terms of negotiating fee-for-service pricing with payers. IPAs waned in popularity, but some were successful and found ways to offer value through combining the clout of numerous organized providers. Typical value-added services of an IPA include credentialing, information technology planning, consulting, and group purchasing assistance as well as creating an effective single voice in dealing with a hospital or health system.

In organizing an IPA, there are numerous strategic questions that must be answered. Perhaps the most important is to outline what you are trying to accomplish, establishing clear and consistent goals that align with the needs of the participants in the IPA. Another important question is whether the local physician community is interested in forming and financially supporting such an organization. While an IPA does not have to be an elaborate or expensive organization, there will be costs to form and operate the entity. Another strategic consideration is governance. If the IPA is formed to principally benefit one specialty over another or is not fairly governed in a balanced way to represent all stakeholders, it will not be politically sustainable. IPAs may be formed around primary care physicians, specialty physicians, or both. If they are to represent both, then an issue to be resolved will be how each constituency is represented on the board or leadership council. In addition to governance, it will be very important from the outset to resolve who will be invited to participate in the organization. Establishing membership criteria is an important aspect of planning. Altering these rules later may be difficult to do, or even politically impossible, so it will be important to "get it right the first time."

If the IPA is being formed around the medical staff of an institution, then privileges at that institution will be an important criteria. Equally helpful will be the support of the institution. If the IPA is being created to enhance the voice of physicians on the medical staff, explaining these reasons to facility leaders will be important. Remember that down the road, you will likely be challenged on your membership criteria if it is not applied consistently and especially if the IPA is successful in its mission such that participation becomes a valuable strategic asset for a practice. IPAs can be a forceful and impactful way to provide value to independent physicians and provide an organized strategy to better align physician groups. It can be an excellent place for hospitals to achieve greater partnerships with the medical staff.

IPAs can be a good model for integration. The IPA can be clinically integrated or financially integrated much like physician hospital organizations (PHOs). This was often the model that was used in the 1990s concept of a "clinic without walls." In this construct, there was financial or clinical integration, but at this time, clinical integration was very difficult because information systems and technology in general were not as sophisticated. Now, moving to one electronic medical record (EMR) or a common health information platform makes it easy to share clinical information, although it is still expensive.

The Physician Hospital Organization: Venus and Mars Form a Company

The title of this section is meant to cause a smile, but it is actually very true. In many cases, the formation of a PHO is done by a hospital or health system and a physician IPA. By its very nature, a PHO is formed by two entities that often have competing goals and incentives. This reality can make a PHO a potentially dysfunctional organization to manage. There are legitimate reasons to form a PHO. It could be formed to facilitate contracting with payers and the development of an accountable care organization (ACO). It could be formed to facilitate information systems development or to improve loyalty to the facility. From the outset, it will be important to determine if the two partners have a good cultural, economic, and strategic fit. If the organizations forming the PHO have a shared vision and established trust, there is likely the foundation for a strong PHO.

PHOs began to be formed in the mid-1980s as an answer to payer requests to negotiate preferred provider organization (PPO) and health maintenance organization (HMO) networks. As a joint venture facility, the PHO would negotiate and hold the hospital and physician contracts with the payer. If an IPA is formed as part of the PHO, it would derive its physician network from the IPA's membership. If there was no IPA ownership of the PHO, then the PHO would hold direct contracts with the individual physicians (or groups). PHOs could, at that time, negotiate and sign contracts and commit large groups of physicians to pricing agreements with payers. In essence, the PHO would leverage the clout of all the MDs and the facility in such negotiations with the goal that both parties would benefit. The PHO collectively bargains using this market power to achieve higher reimbursements for all parties, even smaller physician practices with no individual market power. Because of their success, PHOs grew impactful and powerful. Some held risk contracts with payers, but a majority held basic fee-for-service based contracts.

As PHOs grew in power and importance, many began to offer additional services to physicians and owner hospitals in an attempt to improve their value. Risk contracting became prevalent in the mid-1990s, and PHOs began to look more like insurers, adding claims administration and medical management services. As payers began to shift risk through capitation, PHOs became risk-bearing entities. As the public rejected managed health plans and fee-for-service models returned, PHOs that had pinned their future on risk models went out of business, downsized, or returned to their core set of contracting services.

PHOs were dealt another blow in the mid-1990s as the regulators promulgated rules that stated that IPAs and PHOs could not improve market power for physicians by jointly negotiating prices with payers on behalf of MDs. Regulators required PHOs to implement and use a query system called a "messenger model" that forced each physician group to accept or decline payer offers as individual businesses. PHOs could not use their market power to negotiate with a payer to pay all providers at the same rate.

One of the unintended consequences of the messenger model PHOs is that it gives an advantage to large groups to contract separately and use their leverage for better rates. In this scenario, large groups get paid more than small groups. This makes it difficult for small physician groups to maintain viability and can have the unintended consequence of encouraging the consolidation of ever-larger physician groups. This can have the effect of leveraging more money from the payer. Sometimes, this can occur at the expense of the primary care group's reimbursement.

It is important to recognize that PHOs are a structure, not a strategy, and they are totally dependent on how well they work to make them successful. They require effective governance, a level of trust between hospital and physicians (and physician to physician), and significant infrastructure to be effective. They require strong physician leadership. There are basically three types of PHOs: financially integrated, clinically integrated, and messenger model PHOs. You can see from Figure 4.5 the different activities each one can provide.

Allowed Activities	Financially Integrated PHOs	Clinically Integrated PHOs	Messenger Model PHOs
Negotiate rates	Yes	Yes	No
Negotiate noneconomic terms	Yes	Yes	Yes

Figure 4.5 Allowed activities by PHO model type.

The financially and clinically integrated models have to follow specific Internal Revenue Service regulations and structures to meet legal requirements and in these cases can negotiate rates as well as noneconomic terms with payers.

The messenger model is constructed differently; the PHO can negotiate noneconomic terms but cannot negotiate price. The PHO must distribute or "messenger" the rate offers to each individual physician and can only act as an intermediary with respect to price. In effect, the price is negotiated directly between each provider and the payer.

The clinically integrated PHO is one of the most important models. Physicians must align with each other and the hospital to distinguish them in the market as a group, and this justifies the higher reimbursement by getting improved, measurable clinical outcomes. There are several tests of whether clinical integration exists. These include the following:

■ Mechanisms are in place to monitor and control utilization.
■ Network physicians are truly engaged in this model.
■ Significant investment of capital, both monetary and effort, is made to build the infrastructure.

Because these PHOs can act as a unit without respect to price, the Federal Trade Commission (FTC) has said that these networks must have "real" integration, and the initiatives of the programs must be designed to achieve improvements in healthcare cost, quality, and efficiency. In addition, contracting with health plans must be "reasonably necessary" to achieve these goals. The initiative cannot be a wolf in sheep's clothing.

Many of the successful clinical integration plans have multiple initiatives that include improvement in healthcare cost and quality and the offer of disease management programs focusing on diabetes, generic drugs, hypertension, smoking, and others. These must be of value for the patient, plan, and physicians and should result in some shared savings back to the invested parties.

A significant number of these PHOs have been extremely effective in creating healthcare savings and utilization improvements while improving quality of care. On the other hand, a large number of PHOs failed and were dissolved. As an alignment initiative, the success of a PHO strategy will be determined by where the health system is with its medical staff. If a PHO already exists, there are compelling reasons to strengthen and energize that organization for the future. If the hospital or medical staff never had a PHO, the organization structure may be worth the time and resources if the system faces an aggressive payer community that is committed to pushing the financial risk back to the provider. In addition, the PHO can be an effective vehicle to launch demonstration projects around the patient-centered medical home (PCMH), information technology, and meaningful use efforts and may be a cornerstone to accountable care initiatives.

For a PHO to be successful in the coming environment, it must add value and play a role in aligning incentives. It must offer organizing efficiencies to both its owners and the payers that would not exist otherwise. Operating a PHO can be an expensive venture, and adding cost to an overburdened system is not wise. Nevertheless, a well-organized PHO is an excellent platform to allow physician groups and hospitals to transform the care they render in an organized and jointly governed manner. Among other benefits, the PHO allows for greater physician education and engagement in reform efforts and provides a contractual context to organize more sophisticated risk reimbursement plans. Many believe this is an ideal place for clinical or financial integration.

The PHO model of integration also becomes increasingly important as we see significant shifting of the financing in healthcare. As payment models move toward global capitation via an ACO or other model, the PHO organizational structure can accept risk and achieve significant cost, utilization, and outcome improvements. These cost efficiencies will come at the expense of the hospital from preventable admissions, decreased readmission, and decreased length of stays. Importantly, this changes the hospital from a revenue source to a cost entity. Within this framework, a PHO can serve to share these savings fairly and equally among the hospital and the physicians. Consequently, to achieve cost-efficiency savings, many of the savings will come out of efficiencies and evidence-based care but also by decreasing the amount of highest-cost services delivered that are often hospital based and specialty physician based. To make this model work, this revenue must shift back to all of the participants that are investing capital and "sweat equity." Thus, it makes sense for a PHO to become a distributor of these funds. It may be the perfect vehicle to share risk via bundled payments through ACOs.

Bibliography

Aderholdt, Betsy and Lockridge, Jeff. Partnering with doctors through co-management, *Health Progress*, July–August 2011, http://www.chausa.org/authorindex.aspx?year=2011

American Hospital Association. *Moving health care forward*, January 2011, http://www.aha.org/content/00-10/5barrierstoclininteg.pdf

Arvantes, James. Geisinger Health System reports that PCMH model improves quality, lowers costs", May 26, 2010, http://www.aafp.org/online/en/home/publications/news/news-now/practice-management/20100526geisinger.html

Aston, Geri. Are you ready for physician co-management? August 19, 2011, http://www.hhnmag.com/hhnmag/jsp/articledisplay.jsp?dcrpath=HHNMAG/Article/data/11NOV2010/1110HHN_FEA_clinical&domain=HHNMAG

Bader, Barry S. *Clinically Integrated Physician-Hospital Organizations.* Great Boards, Winter 2009.

Berkson, Doug. Exploring the medical home, expanding to the medical neighborhood (utilizing unwarranted variation as a framework). Spring Managed Care Forum, Orlando, FL, presentation, April 22, 2010.

Blue Cross Blue Shield of Hawaii. *HMSA patient-centered medical home*, http://www.hmsa.com/providers/assets/HMSA_PCMHProgramGuide.pdf

Boomershine, Jeff. *Orthopedic Service Line Co-Management Agreements.* Somerset Health Care Team, Indianapolis, IN, April 12, 2011. jboomershine@somersetCPAs.com

Cohen, Robert. Clinical co-management summary, Kutak Rock LLP, Atlanta, Denver, Des Moines, Fayettteville, Irvine/Los Angeles, Little Rock, Chicago, Scottsdale, Washington, DC, Wichita. www.kutakrock.com/publications/healthcare/CMS053012e.pdf

Cornerstone Alliance. Annual Meeting, December 1, 2009, Lima, OH.

Corrigan, Karen. *The Top 10 in 2010: ten forces framing strategic discussions for health system leaders*, Navvis & Company, March 2010, www.navvisandcompany.com; http://www.slideshare.net/KarenCorrigan/top-10-in-2010

Cox, Kathleen. 7 steps to collaborate with orthopedists on implant costs, Sg2, February 22, 2010 http://members.sg2.com/content-detail-standard/?contentid=7825562542888382473

Elliott, Victoria Stagg. How to seal a co-management deal with a hospital. January 23, 2011. http://www.amednews.com

Evans, Melanie. Co-management emerges as alternative to joint ventures, employment by hospitals. May 10, 2010. http://www.modernphysician.com

Forecast demand by care site and disease timeline, impact of change v10.0: NIS; Pharmetrics: CMS; Sg2 Analysis. 2011. http://www.sg2.com.

Iqbal, Yasmine. How "rules of engagement" can help bridge the divide between surgery and medicine, www.todayshospitalist.com, August 19, 2011 http://www.todayshospitalist.com/index.php?b=articles_read&cnt=145

Mauer, Barbara J. National overview: behavioral health primary care integration and the person-centered healthcare home, National Council for Community Behavioral Healthcare, January 12, 2009.

Medical homes in 2011: one-third to join an accountable care organization", www.HIN.com, April 2011, www.hin.com/lp/hinwkly062711.html

Minich-Ourshadi, Karen. Marking margin with the medical home, September 2011, www.healthleadersmedia.com http://www.healthleadersmedia.com/content/MAG-270678/Making-Margin-with-the-Medical-Home.html

Morreale, Daniel. Multidisciplinary clinical integration for genuine care coordination. Health Access Solutions. http://www.HealthAccessSolutions.com.

Putting it all together, quality improvement and your practice. http://www.doctorsadvocate.org/wpcontent/uploads/2011/05/DoctorsDigest_PuttingItTogether.pdf

Sg2 Staff. *Strategies for hospital-physician integration*, www.sg2.com, September 10, 2008, http://members.sg2.com/contentdetailstandard/?ContentID=2260893

Society of Hospital Medicine's (SHM) Co-Management Advisory Panel. *A Guide to Hospitalist/Orthopedic Surgery Co-Management.*

Chapter 5

Physician Employment

What Is Old Is New: Employment

Anyone involved in healthcare in the 1990s may feel like they are living in a time warp. The 1990s brought us hope that integrated networks, anchored by employed physicians (especially primary care providers) would usher in an age of accountability and efficiency. There were numerous warning signs; this was not to be the case.

First and foremost, hospitals and health systems employed physicians under models that left the parties misaligned. In addition, on the way to Nirvana, no one seemed to ask consumers if they were ready for benefit plans that supported tight management of care. Looking back on those developments, we see these issues more clearly. At the time, many thought employment was the foundation for fundamental change.

One of the problems we got into back in the 1990s was the ultimate payment structure inside the practice. Often, the practice was capitated externally, or the delivery system was capitated externally, encouraging the right incentives from a global basis. However, inside the practice, it was fee-for-service. This happened even more so for delivery systems. While the delivery system was paid a global payment, inside the delivery systems, the physicians were paid on a fee-for-service basis. Thus, the incentives actually never really changed inside the system and forced the system to try to change behavior without changing incentives (Figure 5.1).

As we fast-forward 15 years, the slow motion train wreck of healthcare cost escalation has shown us no sign of abating. Spurred by healthcare reform and the desire for fundamental change, health systems are again entering the employment arena. There are differences this time around. No one doubts that the status quo of healthcare is unsustainable. Driven by reimbursement changes from Medicare, some specialty physicians have seen their ancillary revenues impacted dramatically.

Integration model	Description	Percent of physicians currently aligned via the corresponding model*	Percent of physicians most interested in pursuing the corresponding model over the next 2 years*	Level of alignment
Employment	Physicians are employed for medical services. In return, either a full-time or a part-time salary is paid by a hospital, medical foundation, provider-based clinic, faculty practice plan, or group practice.	44%	46%	High
Joint venture	In a joint venture between physicians and multiple service lines, such as ambulatory surgery and imaging and laboratory centers, the venture owns the service lines and bills third-party payers for patient services.	8%	38%	Medium
Co-manage-ment company	Either by direct contract or through a new-entity joint venture management company, the hospital contracts with physicians to manage a service line. The hospitals and physicians share in the management contract based on their ownership shares.	8%	34%	Medium
Leasing	A hospital, a physician, or a hospital-and-physician joint venture leases space, equipment, or staff for a predetermined time period.	9%	21%	Medium
Directorships, stipends, and management contracts	Services are driven contractually, including leadership and administrative oversight provided by a clinician leader. Some of the responsibilities are certification/education of medical staff and liaising with the medical staff.	24%	51%	Low
No integration	A physician has no financial ties to a hospital, practicing either independently; or at an insurer; or in a group practice, a consulting firm, a government agency, a biotech/pharmaceutical company, or some other organization.	29%	N/A	None

Figure 5.1 Alignment models. (Reprinted with permission from PwC Health Research Institute.)

Access to physicians in jeopardy as rates fall further behind cost increases

- Without congressional action on Medicare physician payment reform, physicians will face a pay cut of about 30 percent, and pay will be held at that level while their practice costs continue to rise.

- This cut comes at a time when Medicare payments for physician services have been nearly frozen for a decade, while the cost of caring for patients has increased by more than 20 percent. After adjusting for inflation, average 2020 Medicare payment rates will be just half of what they were in 2001.

- Access problems would be widespread and affect millions of patients. The baby-boom generation has now started to enroll in Medicare, and the size of the Medicare population is expected to grow from 45 million in 2011 to 58 million by 2020. The 10 million military members and their families covered by the TRICARE program are also affected as, by law, TRICARE rates are limited to Medicare rates.

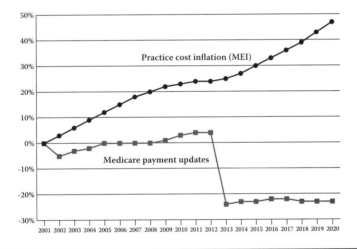

Figure 5.2 Percentage Medicare reimbursement. (© **2012 American Medical Association. All rights reserved. Reprinted with permission.**)

Figure 5.2 details the percentage charge in reimbursement from Medicare over the last number of years. These facts are changing previously successful business models in numerous specialties. In response, many physicians now view employment as a "safe harbor" in the storm of reimbursement changes. Primary care physicians, in particular, are choosing employment at a rapid rate.

From a physician's viewpoint, the current environment is hostile to private practice. Threats of reimbursement reductions, increased practice costs, increased regulatory and information technology (IT) demands have created a tipping point. The stigma that once marked being an employed physician appears to be disappearing.

In reviewing potential employment opportunities, physicians usually desire to maintain as much autonomy and feel of private practice as possible while enjoying the stability of a larger employer. In a marked change from the purchases of the 1990s, health systems are not paying for goodwill and are structuring compensation around productivity with a quality bonus. The heart of the transaction is a valuation of the practice by an outside third party. This determination of "fair market value" ensures that the health system or hospital will only compensate the practice within a narrow range of reasonable value for tangible and intangible assets.

Often, the valuation of the practice is accompanied by an evaluation of operations that outlines the practice's performance against key performance indicators. The Medical Group Management Association (MGMA) has defined benchmarks that are often used to measure practice performance before purchase.

It is important to note that two business transactions are actually taking place. First, the practice assets are being purchased. Second, a physician is being offered an employment agreement. Both transactions have profound legal implications, and both must be done inside the cloak of fair market value.

Another obvious reason to assess the practice at the outset would involve cultural fit of the physician to the organization. If the physician's personal and professional goals do not fit those of the organization, it is likely a harbinger of troubles for the relationship. Cultural fit can be assessed with interviews from outside third parties, reviewing practice literature and procedures, as well as direct discussions between the health system and the physician. (See appendix for cultural fit tool.)

In looking at Figure 5.3, one can see how critical the shared values are; in fact, it is the puzzle piece in the middle. Other things, such as vision, operational support, and the like, are all contributing to the overall fit. Ultimately, the philosophies have to be the same for a long-term successful relationship. Many physicians are jumping into relationships based purely on the initial monetary reward, not thinking through the long-term challenges of working with an entity that may have cultural differences from themselves.

For the average physician contemplating employment, he or she is likely to be calculating the cost/benefit around the concept of required changes compared to perceived value of the new relationship. In such a situation, transparency is your friend. If both parties enter the transaction with eyes wide open and prepared for the contingencies, the possible breakup scenario need not be devastating to either party.

In looking at unwinding provisions of a contract, it is important for both parties to make sure that they can part as friends. Obviously, it becomes critical to both the hospital and the physicians that, should an employment relationship not work, they can continue working together. This may be less critical in a two or more hospital town; however, in most cases, it is best for both parties if the unwinding provision is agreed on in advance and therefore the unwinding is not antagonistic.

The health system behaviors of the 1990s were highly reactionary and, in most cases, hardly disciplined. The frenzy that employment created in the 1990s drove

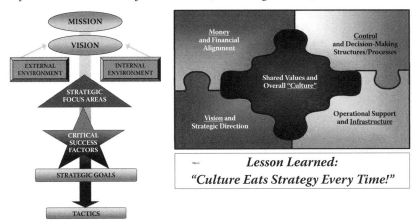

Figure 5.3 Cultural fit. (Reprinted with permission from Navigant Consulting.)

systems to pursue transactions that were not sustainable and not well aligned with the health system's strategies. The transactions were a reaction, not a proactive part of an overall physician alignment plan. It is fair to ask why this scenario is not just repeating itself. There is good evidence that this is not a redo of the 1990s.

This time around, it appears that the parties are coming to similar conclusions at the same time. Hospitals realize that they must offer physicians an opportunity to be more highly integrated because the environment is too hostile to sustain the strategy with a purely voluntary, unaligned medical staff. The freewheeling days of attracting physicians to any town with the belief that "hanging the shingle means success" are over. In this vernacular, creating the positive journey means each party treating the other with respect.

Even as a hospital dives back into these waters, it is likely happening in certain specialties more than others. As Figure 5.4 depicts, employment was more likely in some specialties than others in 2012. Driven by economics, some physicians are changing business models faster than others. Many predict this will continue to evolve. But, even as the pace picks up, more hospitals are entering the employment arena with realistic expectations. In many cases, the "economics" of the transaction may leave the practice losing money. This is more likely true where ancillary services that were part of the practice are moved back to the hospital.

In some of these models, the ancillaries are now moved to hospital billing. This is a temporary model in that now, the patients will be billed from the hospital location

	Specialty*	Percent interested in employment
Most interested in employment	Cardiology	63%
	Psychiatry	61%
	Surgery	53%
	Ob-gyn	50%
	Otolaryngology	50%
	Rheumatology	50%
	Internal medicine	49%
	Emergency medicine	48%
	Pediatrics	48%
Interested in employment	Anesthesiology	48%
	Family medicine	46%
	Dermatology	45%
	Pulmonology	43%
	Endocrinology	39%
	Oncology	39%
	Allergy	38%
	Ophthalmology	38%
Least interested in employment	Neurology	31%
	Radiology	31%
	Nephrology	30%
	Gastroenterology	27%
	Urology	25%
	Orthopedics	25%

* Specialties with fewer than 10 respondents were excluded from the list.

Figure 5.4 Employment by specialty. (Reprinted with permission from PwC Health Research Institute.)

of service when they have ancillary tests in the physician's office. This model, though, in the short run, actually funds the increasing salaries for the physicians.

Employment Considerations

A more accurate view of success would require that reporting on profitability should consolidate hospital and practice expenses, the hospital should adopt an attitude of respectful discussion about future practice needs and ask the doctor to think through what he or she would do "if it was still their money 'fueling the practice.'" From the hospital's perspective, determining whether the practice fits within the health system mission and strategic plan is linked to whether the physician can adapt to become part of a team of clinical leaders whose goal is to move the organization forward, not just a practice. If this can be accomplished in a timely, disciplined way, then the value of the integrated practice will sum to beyond what financial projections indicate. Physician leadership is lacking in many systems today. Using the employment model to help create those leaders is a viable strategy. The critical considerations in employment are

- Financial alignment
- Strategic alignment
- Operational support
- Shared values and culture

In some cases, the practice is responsible for the total profit and loss (P&L) of their practice, an old model with a new face. In this role, the practice has the budgetary responsibilities, and in fact the salary is billings minus the budget or could be work relative value units (WRVUs) minus the budget. Either way, in this scenario, the practice is responsible for managing the practice costs. This gives the physicians much responsibility but also the freedom to hire nurse practitioners and others.

While there are several models of employment in use today, the transaction itself usually involves two separate agreements. The first is the actual employment agreement between the individual doctor and the hospital or physician corporation. The second agreement is the asset purchase agreement, which governs the purchase of practice assets. The engaging health system or hospital will start with a template for both of these agreements. Time and experience will likely alter the agreements as physicians and their attorneys react to the documents. The best advice must be to think through any changes before changing the agreement. It is best not to create an unlevel playing field between different practice purchases and always to use good business logic when you deviate from your template. Treat every change as one that will need to be defended with all other physicians. Being told no to a request to make changes can be respected if the physician understands the reasons, and fairness and sustainability are emphasized. Physicians as well as hospitals fear the repeat of the employment debacle of the 1990s. They know there are no other boats to get into other than the facilities' vessel, and they want it to work. The wise health system will channel these mutual desires in the negotiation process.

It cannot be emphasized enough that hospital buying practices must treat all practices the same. The model and the structures should be similar. Evaluations should use similar tools and benchmarks. Certainly, there are no secrets in healthcare, particularly, in small towns, and any preferential treatment given to a group will soon be learned by other healthcare providers; therefore, ultimate fairness and transparency become critical for a long-term successful model.

Long before the first discussions around agreements, a system needs to answer some fundamental questions about what type of physician relationship it is trying to create. Some systems create a subsidiary or more than one subsidiary to house employed physicians contractually. Do you have one large subsidiary or separate primary care and specialist subsidiaries? There is no perfect answer, but the answer can be tailored to the environment and the strategy needs of the health system. These choices have implications as the system promotes the model. Whatever model is chosen, it is important to be transparent about the goals and objectives of the new organizations and how they will be governed.

Changing World: Making the Decision

Today, there is rapid consolidation of physician practices, and many hospitals are buying practices. This is particularly true for cardiology, oncology, and primary care, although all practices seem to be talking to potential suitors. So then why should a physician consider selling? There are a number of reasons to consider such a transaction, but it is most important not to get caught up in the emotion of the moment. A physician should take time to think and evaluate the pros and cons of selling a practice. Often, it is prudent to stay the course and wait and watch rather than jumping into a poor arrangement. It is definitely prudent to ask questions, talk to people, and make sure both the national environment and the local environment are understood. Many times, it is difficult to be the last one on the market, particularly from the subspecialty side, since often this puts you in a very weak leveraging position in selling your practice.

From a specialist's point of view, any employment agreement needs to be focused on the referral market. From a specialist's point of view, that is the bread and butter and critical piece in maintaining a salary. The specialist should carefully look at where referrals originate currently and in the future and make sure the intended system for alignment can support that specialist being continually busy. If it cannot support that specialist's volume long term, it will not be a successful relationship.

The most important thing is to evaluate all options carefully. Keep talking to leaders in the community so you understand the environment and evaluate your options, getting expert advice if needed. Being naïve and thinking you never have to sell your practice or conversely jumping in to sell your practice in panic is rarely the right option.

Physician Employment Agreements

From the Physician Side

For many physicians, employment is ideal: no more worrying about the business side of medicine, a guaranteed salary, fixed benefit structures, and someone else to manage staff and billing. This can be a wonderful situation for many physicians, some at the beginning of their career and some as they wind down their careers.

There are, however, significant challenges with the agreements between the physician and employers (usually the hospital). These are issues best evaluated with an attorney who has experience in these kinds of agreements. It is important for the physician to read the contract him- or herself since many of these issues are unique to healthcare, and even an experienced lawyer can understand the legal implications but not understand their relationship to the delivery of healthcare. Any perspective physician employee should be particularly aware of several hot spots.

The first one is making sure the job description is accurate. This includes what the job is and in particular links directly to that physician's specialty care. Many specialty physicians may be uncomfortable providing primary care medicine, so the particular type of practice should be carefully spelled out. This should also include the number of hours that should be worked and night call expectations.

One of the hottest items is a noncompete covenant. Many states have guidelines that keep this within certain parameters; however, this can be a major sticking point. The physician should carefully evaluate the noncompete covenant and make sure he or she can abide by it. Many times, the noncompete covenant can be related to a certain mileage or a certain time frame from a specific hospital or clinic location. Sometimes, there is a buyout provision so that if a physician does want to stay and compete, that privilege can be compensated. These things need to be decided up front rather than after the fact, which can be expensive, time-consuming, and emotionally troubling litigation.

One increasing trend is that hospitals are paying sign-on bonuses for stricter and tighter noncompetes. Noncompetes can be loose (e.g., 1 year and several miles) or can be extremely tight, essentially putting the physician in a position to have to move out of town should the relationship unwind. A physician should think long and hard before committing to a strict noncompete agreement even if additional monies are offered up front. There should be a structure for buyout of the noncompete agreement from the physician's side so that some flexibility remains. Once again, a long-term view of any type of employment/employee relationship is critical.

Payment recoupment must be part of the discussion. Physicians should be very careful regarding how salaries are determined and understand any type of bonus or benefit structure. They should also understand any "risk" considerations that might include recoupment of revenues. In addition, the conditions under which the compensation methods can change are important to delineate in the agreement.

Outside activities should also be delineated by physicians who do any speaking or any other additional activities that might add to revenues. It needs to be determined whether these monies go to the employer or to the physician. Things like clinical trials, speaking engagements, writing a book, or locum tenens assignments fall into this category.

Another issue to consider is any type of special work needs. Some physicians do significant mission work either in or out of the country, and it should be negotiated in advance how this will be handled at the practice level.

Discussing tail coverage and understanding malpractice coverage is critical. In most employee agreements, the employer will cover malpractice. The physician should know if this is a "claims-made" policy, which is the usual case, or an "occurrence policy." In a claims-made policy, those claims may not appear for several years; therefore, tail coverage is required on termination. This can be expensive, particularly in some specialties and in some states. An agreement on how this should be handled should be discussed ahead of time and should be included in the contract.

Also, practice governance and the decision-making process should be carefully discussed and understood and put in the contract. How new physicians, nurses, or nurse practitioners will be added to the practice and how this will be handled financially should be documented.

It is important that the management and control of the practice decisions be discussed in advance, including how much decision making physicians will actually have and who will be on the board or leadership council to control this decision making. This is particularly important concerning how the budgets will be made and set, who will have the authority to add or hire new physicians, whether competing groups will be allowed into the model, and other considerations.

This is a complex process that should be evaluated carefully with expert opinions sought.

From the Hospital Side

Why do hospitals to want to acquire practices? To some, it does not seem to make sense since, traditionally, hospitals have typically lost money on purchased practices. Well, the answer is different for different systems. In general, however, hospitals feel that they can create downstream revenue from referrals that generate from a practice that should more than make up for any operating loss. This is particularly true with primary care, which tends to direct patients for diagnostic testing, specialty consultations, and inpatient care. In most primary care practices, hospitals have lost money. This will likely continue. However, in the past the downstream cost failed to make up for many of these losses. It remains to be seen if influencing the starting point in care will pay off. The specialty world is different. Most of the current strategy of hospitals is to transfer the ancillary services to hospital-based services. This means that diagnostic and other technical components will be billed on the hospital side (Figure 5.5). The reimbursement tends to be higher, and this gives the hospital increased revenue to spend on supporting physicians' salaries. There is concern that this might not be a long-term model since this not only increases the cost of healthcare to the employer or payer but also usually adds cost to the individual patients since, typically, the copays and coinsurance are higher when paying at a site of service that is labeled "hospital."

While this model of increased ancillary cost is a temporary model, having all these specialists, primary care, and other providers in the family becomes a critical piece to providing integrated care. Integrated care should lead to increasing efficiencies, which then should cost less to the payer and patient and should lead to an effective healthcare management model (Figure 5.6).

There are also good defensive reasons for hospitals buying practices. If competing hospitals are buying practices that could potentially isolate referrals from your system, buying practices simply to prevent the other system from locking in referrals is a prudent idea. This, of course, can be dangerous if the price points rise to the "irrational" level at which hospitals are paying overinflated prices for these practices that they will never earn back in operating revenue. This can create issues like we had in the 1990s when hospitals bought practices at irrational prices.

Physician View

There are many things physicians should consider when selling a practice. The first and most important is the culture fit to the system. Is the physician willing to be an employee of a system? This gives considerably less freedom in coming and going and making financial decisions. It is critical that the culture of the system is compatible with the physician's values. Culture needs should be considered as well as personality types. The physician must be willing to sacrifice some autonomy for the guarantees and safety that come with being an employee. Of course, many physicians are fatigued with the role of practice leader and are quite willing to turn over the reins to the hospital. One consideration is how much longer the physician plans to work. This transition can be a great strategy in guaranteeing salary and protecting a falling income. It can also increase nonfinancial benefits and be a stable way of moving toward retirement. From the hospital side, it should be looking to bring in younger physicians to the practice to help transition the practice over the next couple of years to make a win-win for everybody. In this case, the senior physician must be willing to act as a mentor.

One must also consider the local market environment. In primary care, you are most likely okay in going it alone for a while, although it will be increasingly difficult to run an efficient practice in a small group with larger groups and hospitals running practices that are competing with you. However, in an area that has limited primary care access, as many areas in the country experience, there is still a market for primary care practices to "watch and wait."

Specialists are in a different position. In many areas of the country, there is an overabundance of specialists. One thing that must be looked at is where your specialty group sits in relation to the community. If another large specialty group sells to a single-town, single-hospital system, you could be in a difficult position. Conversely, if that hospital owns a number of primary care physicians and then buys a competing specialty practice, your referrals could go away with the contract signature. So, from the specialty side, the issue would be making sure that your referral sources are stable, and this requires making sure that any primary care or other direct referral sources are in the same system that you are or that being independent does not sacrifice those relationships.

Medical Group	*Hospital*
• Monthly charges, collections, adjustments	• Average length of stay
• Aged accounts receivable	• Bed occupancy
• Gross and net collection rates	• Net patient revenue
• Total A/R and days in A/R	• Operating margin
• Productivity	• Debt service coverage
• Actual vs. scheduled hours	• Current ratio
• No shows and cancellations	• Cash on hand
• RVUs	• Accounts receivable (days)
• Average weeks worked/year	• Accounts payable
• Clinical hours/week	
• Ambulatory and hospital encounters	

Figure 5.5   Medical group metrics and hospital metrics. (From Fabrizio, N., MGMA Health Care Consulting Group, 2001. With permission.)

• Telling the physicians that they are not required to make a profit
• Hospital strips out ancillaries
• Hospital overhead allocated to the group
• Office staff on hospital's salary and benefits
• No capable physician leader in place
• Productivity standards not in place
• No downside risk in compensation
• Lack of physician participation in governance, management and budgeting (and no ownership)
• No critical mass of employed physicians
• No group organization (physicians sharing a tax ID)
• Inexperienced managers

Figure 5.6   Revisiting practice acquisition purchases, proven ways to fail. (Courtesy of Ken Mack, FACHE, president of Ken Mack and Associates.)

Selling Your Medical Practice: Pros & Cons	
Staying a Private Practice	*Selling to Hospital System*
Advantages	
Make your own decisions, therefore, decision making can be straightforward and swift.	Support from other hospital departments, HR, IT/EMR Accounting, Reimbursement, Collections, Compliance, Insurance, etc.
Practice can be nimble in response to changing medical landscape.	Potential to climb into other administrative positions.
Put your mark on the practice and be more creative.	Interact with managers of other departments/broaden knowledge and understanding of the care continuum.
Private practice owners usually take a salary draw, split any receipts after all expenses are paid and generally distribute receipts monthly.	Eliminates concerns about the financial viability of the practice. Guaranteed salary, regular hours, paid benefits/vacation are benefits.
In control of your own destiny and have professional independence and administrative control.	Providing healthcare is becoming increasingly complex. Keeping up with regulations from insurers, the governments, transitioning to EMR, etc., provide challenges.
Disadvantages	
Could have physicians in your practice who may not have business expertise and may fight you on decisions.	You can expect much less autonomy in a hospital system, and there will be red tape involved in getting even simple requests filled.
Can learn a lot from the process or preparing for and living through a JCAHO visit.	Hospital can be in panic mode getting ready for JCAHO visits.
Physicians may make less money every time a new non-revenue generating position is added, or equipment is replaced.	It can be frustrating to balance the needs of your staff and the hospital.

continued

Selling your Medical Practice: Pros & Cons (continued)	
Staying a Private Practice	*Selling to Hospital System*
Disadvantages (continued)	
No internal career path.	Because the hospital is the number one priority, the needs of the clinics may be down in the line of importance.
Ever increasing administrative and regulatory burdens.	Contractual negotiations—many items to consider.
Younger physicians are demanding a more manageable work week and work/life balance. This may have implications for physician recruitment.	Productivity targets can be overwhelming; practice expenses to which you are being held, but over which you have no control can be an issue.
Supporting a new physician increases risk and profits.	What will you do if it does not work out in the long run? What changes to contract upon renewal? Do you have a Plan B?

Considering Hospital Employment? You should understand................
Contract Terms
• Who is the ultimate decision maker relative to practice issues and who would they report to?
• Termination provisions should be clearly spelled out. If possible, negotiate terms that make it difficult for the hospital to terminate, but relatively easy for the physician to end employment.
• The agreement survives changes in hospital ownership.
• Be aware of and understand any restrictive covenant or noncompete clauses. These are the most frequent source of litigation related to MD termination of hospital employment.
Compensation
• Negotiate a substantial guaranteed base salary over a long period of time regardless of productivity.
• If an incentive bonus is offered, know how it is calculated. If based on RVUs, the RVU value should be locked in with the contract is signed.
• On-call time—if compensated, contract could specify a definite number of call days per month.

Selling your Medical Practice: Pros & Cons (continued)
Staff, Facilities, Resources
• Specify the staff provided (include details on training, salary range, etc.) exact nature of facilities and the resources that will be available.
Hiring and Firing
• Have the final say in hiring and the option to fire staff.
New Physician Hires
• Negotiate say in process.
Benefits
• Vacation time, educational leave, insurance coverage (medical disability, life, malpractice) payment of professional dues, etc., all need to be negotiated and included in the contract.
• Regarding malpractice insurance, will they continue your existing coverage (and retroactive date), purchase an extended reporting endorsement ("tail" coverage)? If agreement terminates by either party, does all past exposure lie with the hospital?
Practice Appraisal
• How much is your practice worth?
• You might want to engage the services of a practice valuation professional to assist you.
Ask yourself these questions................
• How does your practice philosophy fit with the hospital's care philosophy?
• How does your practice fit into the hospital's strategic plan?
• Do you really "need" to sell your practice?
• If you sell your practice, what will change? Is this acceptable?
• Will the hospital's IT work for your practice?
• Are financial expectations clear?
• What has changed since the last rush to physician employment in the 1990s? Have hospitals learned how to manage practices?
• Where will you be in three years? Be prepared for changes when the contract is up for renewal.

It Is All About Integration

In the end, it is all about integration. No matter who owns which practices, or systems, system practices will eventually refer to other system practices if there are any, and ultimately, clinical integration and passing of patient-level information and appropriate referrals back and forth with good information flow should improve patient outcomes. At the same time, it should decrease the cost of individual healthcare. This is ultimately the goal of all of these strategies.

where

Foundation Model

The foundation model is often used in communities where law prohibits the direct employment of physicians by health systems or hospitals. The foundation is typically a not-for-profit entity that is a subsidiary of the health system or facility. The foundation usually owns and operates physician practices (including the office facilities) and often employs all nonphysician staff. It is likely to be responsible for all business infrastructure needs, including IT and financial operations. Physicians, on the other hand, are often contracted to the foundation through an agreement with the remaining physician-owned entity or group practice but are not employees of the foundation. The foundation entity covers all the overhead of operations and collects for the services provided by the physicians. The foundation also takes all the risk for clinic operations, although an agreement with the physicians can vary the reimbursement rate based on clinic performance. Other reasons that a foundation model might be used would include the desire of the physician to stop short of full employment in an alignment initiative.

Creating the foundation model often involves similar transactions of employment as practice assets are sold to the hospital, and the practice is left with income that is solely from selling professional services to the foundation. Foundation model initiatives must meet all of the same legal requirements regarding fair market value.

Physician Service Agreements

Physician service agreements or professional service agreements (PSAs) are the mechanism by which physician groups or an individual physician can contract with a hospital or foundation to be reimbursed for professional services. Often these arrangements are based on a work relative value unit (RVU) model that determines total compensation to a group or individual based on accumulated w/RVUs as units of service. These agreements can take several variations depending on whether the facility or hospital is leasing the physician's services only or expanding the "lease" to include physician practice support staff. In some cases, a lease of the facilities that support the practice accompanies the lease of professional services. This is often the case if the facility is cash-strapped or the physicians are not ready to sell their infrastructure. The amount for which the professional services are purchased or leased by the hospital must meet all fair market value tests similar to other alignment contracts.

Clinical Institutes

PHO

A clinical institute is an organizational structure developed by the hospital or health system that creates a member-based organization around professional cooperation and agreement on clinical principles and evidenced-based medicine. A clinical institute is usually open to any member of the medical staff as long as the physician adheres to the care principles of the institute. Often, a charter and agreement are developed whereby the institute member accepts responsibility to practice evidenced-based medicine, assist in the development of clinical protocols, ensure data sharing and transparency to advance best practice, and promote collegial behavior. Clinical institutes have aligning features around practice style, care pathways, and outcomes but generally have no direct financial impact on the practice or physician income.

Governance

Governance is more likely to be determined by ownership structures and percentages more closely than any other variables. Acknowledging this, any type of joint effort among physicians and hospitals should rely on as much joint governance as is legally possible. For a facility aligned with a group of physicians who are committed to making changes that significantly improve the value of healthcare services to the patient, there should be no fear in sharing governance with physicians. Some alignment initiatives, such as clinical comanagement and the development of a physician hospital organization (PHO) are built around the concept of joint governance. The governance structure of a clinical co-management arrangement is legally mandated so that the management company, a joint venture, must be the entity placed at risk for performance. In a PHO, legal requirements usually dictate that the cost burden of operating the organization must match the ownership of the entity. Therefore, if a physician entity owns half the PHO, it must bear half the burden of the operating expenses. In the case of an independent practice association (IPA), governance is more likely to be led by physicians who participate and usually own the IPA independent of a facility, even if it is built around medical staff privileges at a facility.

Governance itself is obviously about more than just who pays the bills. Inherent in the creation of operating agreements and charters are the issues of board composition and representation, how decisions will be made for the organization, which decisions are operational versus strategic, how disagreements will be settled, and a definition of due process related to membership. The message and operational aspects of governance are also about the message that the governance structure sends about the nature of the organization. Some organizations have boards that allow any members to be present at a board meeting. Transparency and communication are key concepts that governance can impact. The greater the desire for shared sacrifice and effort, the greater effort the board or oversight function should take to help ensure balance and representation.

Whether we are talking about the governance of a PHO or that of a clinical integration effort, we are likely talking about oversight of clinical and business efforts that will require hospital and physician representatives to serve on the oversight group. Picking the right leaders is a major issue that will have an impact on the future success of the organization—choose carefully and strategically. For physicians, a key perspective will be choosing physicians who will be willing to extend the time and energy to participate and offer solutions to the complex issues and remain dispassionate enough to offer a balanced judgment. If a physician or hospital administrator were interviewing for this role in 2012, the individual would definitely need to share the view that the current healthcare system is deeply flawed and we must replace it with an enhanced and more efficient version. A real issue for both of these candidates would be whether he or she had the ability to divorce him- or herself from their typical role and look at the complex issues and solutions as a board member or committee member reviewing specifically the task at hand. Sadly, many a board member brings to the organizational governance process the singular prism of how it will have an impact on his or her practice or department.

Another issue worth considering is the use of patient representatives on the oversight board of the alignment initiative. Patient advocacy representatives can add tremendous insight to the practical and human aspects of alignment initiatives, especially those that involve changes in the manner or quality of direct patient access to caregivers and support staff. While most hospitals are becoming more familiar with the role of patient advocacy in both operational advice and strategic initiatives, physicians and physician organizations have been slower to adopt advocacy models that embrace the patient. In a recent MGMA survey of primary care practices, less than 16% of practices utilized patients in a formal advisory capacity, although for those with a primary care medical home designation it was over 39%. Clearly, thinking about where patient advocacy can fit in your governance model will add value as you seek to align your initiatives with the needs and wants of patients.

Another potential addition to your governance structure could involve the creation of a payer representative position to help govern your alignment initiative. If the initiative is centered on a singular payer relationship, as it could be in an accountable care organization (ACO) development, the payer could be an implicit addition to the oversight board or committee. If, however, the information shared with the board or strategic decision made by the board spans numerous payer relationships, a payer representative may not be appropriate.

Regardless of the makeup of the oversight board, it is important to review and discuss the options and implications prior to the creation of the initiative. Fixing the governance later is never a good idea, and by that point, ideas and attitudes may be hardwired and difficult to change. In addition, choose your leaders wisely and seek out those who can see beyond their own self-interest.

Physician Payment Models

In the physician employment arena, there are multiple payment models that are available. There is no one payment model that meets all needs. In any given employment situation, a combination of different payment models is often used. The following payment models are not meant to be all inclusive but provide a framework of options based on the most important issues.

There are two main types of payment models: fixed and variable. The fixed models are the traditional models utilized in the 1990s; physicians were paid on a salary basis. This model could also be amended to include either capitation or global risk, which has some components of a fixed-fee structure. If the MD compensation is divorced from productivity, it may create friction. The salary model may be the easiest model to administer; however, the risk in this model is both underincentivizing the physician to put in the hours and potentially incentivizing physicians to overutilize excessive referrals. This was one of the issues with capitation in the 1990s that had to be closely monitored.

Newer payment models are often based on both volume and incentives. In this case, the metric can be on total billings or total allowable charges. These models encourage both a high work ethic and increased volume. Other variations of this model can be based on total collections, or some of the newer models use work RVUs as a measure of productivity, and the price is contractually set per work RVU. This model can be weighted to each payer, or it can be neutral in that any work RVU is the same as any other work RVU (regardless of payer mix). This can encourage different patient and insurance mixes but can be a problem if a lower-paying insurer becomes predominant. Lowering collections will make it difficult to pay the bills. This can be the model that is used in mission-based systems in that it encourages the physician to see every patient no matter what the payer source is.

A variation of this is a work RVU model based on weighted RVUs by payer. This takes into account the different payment rates and can encourage the physician to see higher-paying patients more than other patients or, at least, compensate for some of the payment differentials.

In other payment models, payments can be based on outcomes and *quality*. These are often added to the fixed- or variable-incentive models related to a defined percentage of total compensation. The percentage can be as low as 10% but in some systems can approach 50%. These models are similar to pay-for-performance programs that many managed care companies are using.

The quality scores can be based on multiple factors, such as HEDIS (Health Employer Data Information Set) measures or other evidence-based care scores that are mutually agreed on. It is difficult to measure actual outcomes at the practice level, but eventually outcomes with morbidity and mortality will be measured. In addition, utilization or total patient cost can be measured as a proxy of efficiency and effectiveness. This can be based on dollars or utilization (in either the outpatient or the inpatient arena) as well as total length of stay in the hospital. This model only works in a population-based program where there are enough patients to obtain accurate metrics. It is also possible to carve out certain outliers from this measurement to be fair to all.

The last item in this outcome measure is satisfaction "scores." This can be patient satisfaction scores based on their perception of quality of care, waiting time, office staff, and so on. Satisfaction scores can be a longitudinal review of patent satisfaction with downstream referral partners as well, including scores from the referring physicians.

Patient satisfaction can also be extended to medical directors, hospital personnel, and others. Other physician-hospital alignment strategies can also be included in the incentives, such as clinical co-management projects, service line management, creating protocols to improve efficiencies within the hospital, or other things that align with the hospital systems' strategic initiatives.

One other important payment strategy is proxy RVUs or hourly payment rates for nonclinical services. The physicians can be reimbursed for services that are not directly related to patient care. These may be administrative services or

Fixed	• Salary
	• Capitation
	• Global risk
Volume incentive	• Billings total
	• Billings allowable
	• Collections
	• Work RVUs, total fixed
	• Work RVUs, weighted by payer
Outcomes/quality	• Quality scores
	• Satisfaction scores
	• Utilization/patient costs

Figure 5.7 Physician payment models.

nonreimbursed clinical services. These can be paid using proxy RVUs, which are paid at an agreed-on rate of compensation per RVUs. These payments can also be in the form of hourly based payments and might include items such as drive time when traveling to another clinic or other agreed-on nonclinical activities.

Essentially, there are multiple variations of payment models (Figure 5.7) that exist in our current healthcare system. This discussion was not meant to be all inclusive but to provide a framework to analyze options. We are rapidly moving from the fixed-payment model to the variable-payment model and ultimately to a value-based payment model. This is based on a combination of quality outcomes, utilization measures, and volume incentives. As we move toward the system of global capitation, these payment models have to continue to be modified to provide incentive for physicians to create value, not volume. In all the payment models, measures must be obtained to ensure that the best care is being delivered, in the right setting, at the right time.

Appendix: Cultural Assessment Tool*

The Physician Engagement Difficulty Assessment is designed to prompt hospital leaders to think carefully about the current structural and historical factors in the organization that will inform the degree of difficulty the hospital might have in moving together with the medical staff to a higher level of partnership for quality and safety.

Score your hospital on each of the seven dimensions. Lower scores indicate an easier environment in which to engage physicians; higher scores indicate a more difficult environment in which to engage physicians. The lowest possible total score is 7; the highest possible total score is 25.

1. Physician connectedness. . . . . Score: _____
   The majority of active staff physicians are:
   ☐ Employed: **score 1**
   ☐ Affiliated (e.g., part-time with the faculty practice plan; in the system network or PPO): **score 2**
   ☐ Independent: **score 3**

2. Physician loyalty. . . . . Score: _____
   The majority of active staff physicians:
   ☐ Are employed by the hospital: **score 1**
   ☐ Admit primarily to this hospital: **score 2**
   ☐ Are splitters (e.g., go to multiple hospitals): **score 3**

3. Stability of medical staff structures, mergers, and relationships. . . . . . Score: _____
   ☐ The medical staff culture has been stable for years: **score 1**
   ☐ The medical staff was merged from more than one facility some years ago and most of the disagreements are over, although there are still some bruised feelings in a few departments: **score 2**
   ☐ The medical staff includes a recent merger, and the wounds are still raw: **score 3**

4. Currency of medical staff bylaws . . . . Score: _____
   The medical staff bylaws reflect current reality:
   ☐ The medical staff bylaws are dynamic, up-to-date, and reflect the current reality: **score 1**
   ☐ The medical staff bylaws were revised in some substantial measure within the last few years to reflect current reality: **score 2**
   ☐ The medical staff bylaws have not been amended or revised in years: **score 3**

* Physician Engagement Difficulty Assessment Tool from Appendix A and IHI white paper

5. **Medical Executive Committee (MEC) authority** . . . . Score: _____
   - ☐ Balanced: The MEC functions effectively as the "Supreme Court" for the staff, and resolves inter-departmental feuds. There is a procedural assumption by the medical staff that the MEC acts fairly and wisely: score 1
   - ☐ The MEC "represents" the medical staff. The board of directors and administration are wary of ceding too much power to the MEC, so the board has the power (occasionally used) to approve/disapprove medical staff officers and department chairs. The Credentials Committee reports to the board and not to the MEC: score 2
   - ☐ Civil libertarian: The emphasis of the MEC is on protecting individual physician rights and maintaining high levels of due process even for minor disciplinary actions. Reactive and formalistic, the MEC rarely initiates any actions that would impinge on the autonomy of individual medical staff members: score 3

6. **Board engagement with medical staff in quality initiatives** . . . . Score: _____
   - ☐ The board engages directly with medical staff, actively seeks staff input, and involves them in all quality initiatives at the earliest stages: score 1
   - ☐ The board watches quality from a distance and depends on administration's reports for monitoring and surveillance of the medical staff: score 2
   - ☐ The board thinks quality of care is purely a medical staff responsibility. There is no real will, no real engagement on the part of the board: score 3

7. **Historic cultural engagement** . . . . Score: _____
   The culture of engagement for physicians is best described as:
   - ☐ Full engagement: Most of the active staff involved in inpatient work participate in initiating, implementing, and improving quality initiatives. The community-based physicians who never come to the hospital are engaged in hospital quality initiatives as they relate to the continuum of care (e.g., appropriateness of admissions, presentation to ER, etc.). The administration is seen as a helpmate and assists in responding to medical staff programs. Interdisciplinary team projects are the norm; the CEO's salary and/or bonus depends on quality results; the board supports physician engagement with resources and education: score 1

Bibliography

AAFP (American Academy of Family Physicians). Find the Value of Your Practice. Accessed June 14, 2011 from www.aafp.org

AAFP (American Academy of Family Physicians). Refine results for selling practice to hospital. Accessed June 14, 2011 from www.aafp.org,

AAFP (American Academy of Family Physicians). Selling Your Practice. 2012. http://www.aafp.org/online/en/home/practicemgt/mgmt/selling.html

Accenture. Clinical transformation: dramatic changes as physician employment grows, 2011. http://www.accenture.com/us-en/Pages/insight-clinical-transformation-physician-employment-grows.aspx and http://www.accenture.com/SiteCollectionDocuments/PDF/Accenture_Clinical_Transformation.pdf

The Advisory Board, Strategy-aligned physician compensation plans, 2009. http://www.advisory.com/Research/Health-Care-Advisory-Board/Studies/2009/Strategy-Aligned-Physician-Compensation-Plans

Alexander, Ian J. The physician as employee: pros and cons. Accessed June 9, 2011 from http://www.aaos.org/news/aaosnow/sep09/managing4.asp

Fu, Richard N. Adapting to a new model of physician employment, http://www.accenture.com/SiteCollectionDocuments/PDF/Accenture-Outlook-Physician-Trends-August-2011-No2.pdf

Huizenga, Mark. 3 things every physician needs to know before selling their practice, Accessed May 2, 2011 from Practice Management Blog, http://www.huizenga-consulting.com/practice-management-blog/?Tag=Physician%20selling%20practice

Jain, Manoj. Hospitals taking over private practices, The Commercial Appeal, Accessed February 14, 2011 from http://www.commercialappeal.com/news/2011/feb/14/hospitals-taking-over-from-private-practices/

Kane, Leslie and Sanders, Jay. Make your practice successful despite today's challenges: join, merge, or sell your practice to a hospital? Accessed January 27, 2010 from WebMD Professional, www.medscape.com also available at http://www.medworm.com/rss/search.php?qu=practice+management&r=Exact&podcasts=on&o=r

Kirchheimer, Barbara. Physician-hospital alignment. http://beckersorthopedicandspine.com/news-analysis/item/1147-to-sell-or-not-to-sell-a-guide-for-orthopedic-practices-eyeing-deals-with-hospitals

Kocher, Robert and Sahni, Nikhil R. Hospitals' race to employ physicians – the logic behind a money losing proposition, *The New England Journal of Medicine*, May 12, 2011. http://www.nejm.org/doi/full/10.1056/NEJMp1101959

Leahy, Maureen. Is a hospital alliance in your future? American Academy of Orthopaedic Surgeons, Accessed June 9, 2011 from http://www.aaos.org/news/aaosnow/mar11/managing5.asp

Majdi, Christopher. Selling a medical practice to a hospital. Transition Consultants. Accessed June 30, 2010 from http://transition-consultants.blogspot.com

MGMA (Medical Group Management Association) survey of primary care practices, http://www.mgma.com/store/Surveys-and-Benchmarking/Cost-Survey-for-Primary-Care-Practices-2010-Report-Based-on-2009-Data-Print-Edition/

MGMA (Medical Group Management Association) Highlights of MGMA's 2011 Physician Compensation survey, http://mgma.com/blog/Highlights-of-MGMAs-2011-Physician-Compensation-survey/

Plaisance, Noah, MGMA 2012 Status and Prospects Report, http://www.mgmaconnexion.com/connexion/201201?pg=44#pg44

Reece, Richard, MD. Wednesday, March 3, 2010. Hospitals and Doctors, Physician Business Ideas; Physician Employment by Hospitals http://medinnovationblog.blogspot.com/2010/03/physician-employment-by-hospitals.html.

Reese, Shelly M. Physician-hospital employment: gaining ground, but what's beyond the bend? Accessed June 17, 2010 from http://www.medscape.com/viewarticle/722058

Reinersten, James L., Institute for Healthcare Improvement, Building a better business case for quality: innovative payment methods, http://www.uft-a.com/PDF/Pages5_9.pdf

Reinersten, James L., Alice G. Gosfield, William Rupp, and John W. Whittington. *Engaging Physicians in a Shared Quality Agenda*. Innovation Series white paper. Cambridge, MA: Institute for Healthcare Improvement, 2007. Available at http://www.IHI.org

Rentel, Victoria. Hospital practice can come with pitfalls for doctors, Accessed June 9, 2011 from http://www.kevinmd.com/blog/2010/04/hospital-practice-pitfalls-doctors.html

Rodriguez, Todd. Should you Consider Selling your Practice to a Hospital? Accessed May 20, 2009 from http://physicianlaw.foxrothschild.com/2009/05/articles/practice-management/should-you-consider-selling-your-practice-to-a-hospital/

Terry, Ken. *Physicians try to come in from the cold*, BNET Industries, December 8, 2008, Business Intelligence Service, Trends & Analysis.

Whaley, Mary Pat. Pros and cons of private or hospital owned practice. Accessed June 9, 2011 from http://www.kevinmd.com/blog/2011/-5/pros-cons-private-hospital-owned-practice.html

Chapter 6

Clinical Integration

Most physicians are in small practices. No matter what happens in healthcare reform, that would not change anytime soon. Clinical integration connects the dots and enables these physicians to meet the needs of the community.

Lee Sacks, MD
President, Advocate Physician Partners

At this point, we have discussed many different models of physician and hospital integration. These all have in common new clinical and financial structures; however, structure itself is insufficient to obtain greater efficiencies in healthcare delivery. To get the necessary level of efficiency requires a patient-centric approach with good financial information flow, good clinical information flow, and integration and alignment of services. It also requires seamless transitions of care and robust communication among caregivers.

Employment of physicians is only one means to this end. It simply lets the physician and the hospital align one another on a financial basis; it does not, however, set up clinical pathways, and it does not necessarily increase information flow across care groups. Employment is simply a structure that is supportive of integration.

Clinical integration is the key to healthcare reform. Everything else in healthcare reform is supportive. Integration must

1. Improve quality.
2. Decrease cost.
3. Improve patient experience.

This is the definition of the IHI (Initiative of Healthcare Improvement) Triple Aim. With these items in mind, payment reform will happen, driven by a number of factors. Ultimately, there are too few dollars to support the healthcare infrastructure and projected growth. We must have better integration of the care delivery system and better transitions of care to create more effective care.

There are four factors that are driving forces:

1. The cost of healthcare is under scrutiny; it is just too expensive.
2. Technologies like electronic health records (EHRs), health information exchanges (HIEs) (a way of connecting different practices), and regional health information organizations (RHIOs) are all making clinical integration a possibility.
3. Physicians are migrating to larger practices (as well as hospital employment), allowing for further integration.
4. The new era of accountability and accountable care organizations (ACOs) is arriving.

The focus here is on population healthcare management and keeping patients in the ambulatory setting. Hospital medical staff models are being reinvented to support this innovation.

With integrated clinical care (Figure 6.1), evidence suggests that spending can be reduced without rationing services. Studies have shown 15–25% of patients who are discharged from the hospital will be readmitted within 30 days; this is unacceptable. This is but one example of waste that can be mitigated with closer outpatient follow-up. Many of these readmissions are preventable.

Other focuses of integration will be to eliminate unnecessary testing, to use procedures that are evidence based, and to facilitate the movement of patients across the care continuum with accurate information and decision support, making for higher-quality/cost-effective care. What we are talking about is not a single event but a well-managed patient care process.

A typical Medicare beneficiary sees a median of two primary care physicians and five specialists collectively working in four different geographical locations. A typical patient with multiple chronic conditions, as it is becoming more typical of our elderly population, has three primary care physicians and eight different specialists in seven different settings. It is truly overwhelming to expect good, consistent care can be developed without an organized care process and effective information transitioned across all providers.

Many patients actually use a specialist as a primary care physician. They can either have one specialist act as their primary care physician or, often, have five or six different specialists and no actual primary care or coordinating physician. This model is often worrisome because, many times, each specialist thinks the other is taking care of some of the basic needs, and often care coordination, basic preventive care, and routine disease management can be missed in this fragmented model.

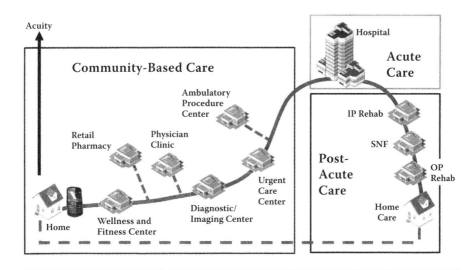

Figure 6.1 Our task for the new order: building a system of CARE that performs. CARE, Clinical Alignment and Resource Effectiveness; IP, inpatient; OP, outpatient; SNF, skilled nursing facility. (From Confidential & Proprietary © 2012 Sg2. Reprinted with permission.)

In addition, there is a real push toward better outpatient care. The hospital, which has typically been the "center of care," is positioning itself by employment of physicians to move into the outpatient space. The focus will be to keep patients out of the hospital by keeping them well and healthy. Eliminating readmissions and emergency room visits by providing preventive care and good alternative access points will also be critical (Figure 6.2).

What Is Clinical Integration?

There are many different definitions of clinical integration. They all focus on collaboration among healthcare providers and geographical locations pushing for higher-quality, better-coordinated, and more efficient care outcomes at a lower cost. One definition of integration is "clinical integration facilitates the coordination of patient care across conditions, providers, settings and time in order to achieve care that is safe, timely, effective, efficient, equitable, and patient-focused" (Health for Life Expert Advisory Group on Clinical Integration) (Figure 6.3).

As stated previously, one of the key enablers of clinical integration is the blossoming of the healthcare information technology infrastructure. This is supported by the HITECH (Health Information Technology for Economic and Clinical Health) Act of 2011 and the push toward meaningful use (and the government's

% of Patients Discharged to Each PAC Site

30-Day Readmissions

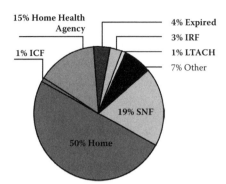

	% of Total Readmits	30-Day Readmit %	30-Day Readmit Index
Home	54.95%	9.88%	0.92
Skilled Nursing	18.77%	18.07%	1.27
Nursing Home	0.36%	16.65%	1.18
Home Health	19.74%	16.40%	1.26
Inpatient Rehab	2.36%	10.46%	0.092

Figure 6.2 What we know: Poorly coordinated postacute care increases readmission rates. IRF, inpatient rehabilitation facility; LTACH, long-term care acute care hospital; PAC, postacute care; SNF, skilled nursing facility. (From 2008 Medicare Claims Date; Sg2 Analysis, 2011.)

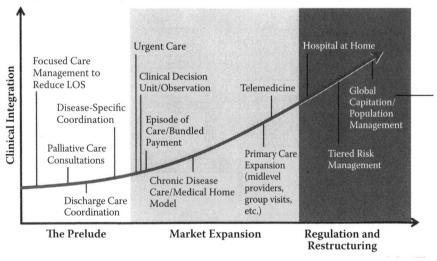

Figure 6.3 Care redesign will occur in a stepwise pattern. LOS, length of stay. (From Confidential & Proprietary © 2012 Sg2. Reprinted with permission.)

financial support of this endeavor). Information technology is critical to delivering appropriate patient information into the right setting.

Payment reforms will happen regardless of healthcare reform and are already happening. Payment reforms do not require legislative input but can be done through a market-based system that includes the Centers for Medicare and Medicaid Services (CMS) and Medicaid services. Major payment reforms that are already happening are helping to support clinical integration. The following are three models that MedPAC (Medicare Payment Advisory Commission) has already suggested:

- Patient-centered medical homes
- Bundling of care episodes
- Accountable care organizations

Bundled Payments

Bundled payments are another method of aligning incentives between healthcare providers. Bundled payment methods are in their infancy; however, in concept, they have been around for some time. They are also referred to as *episode-based payments.*

Bundled payments are a mechanism that a payer can use to align the interests of different providers. As an example, a commercial payer or Medicare pays a single lump sum to an entity such as a hospital, PHO (physician hospital organization), or a group of physicians, and that entity then distributes those payments to all providers involved in the care of that particular patient's episode of care. For example, if we are referencing a total joint replacement for a patient, then the payment might be made to a group of orthopedic physicians, who would be responsible for paying everybody who is involved in the care of that patient from the preoperative period, which includes physician visits and some preoperative physical therapy; to the hospital visit; the surgery (which would include anesthesiologist, radiologist, pathologist, etc.); and often postoperative care. This bundled payment would also be expected to cover a period of time after the surgery, which might include up to 90 days or longer. During this period, should there be a surgical complication requiring readmission or increased medical care, this would also be covered under that original bundled payment.

This can be an extremely complex process depending on what the bundled payment is expected to cover and the entity handling the payment. Negotiating the payment rates for all involved providers can be tricky, particularly as you encounter providers who are providing relatively small levels of care for such individual patients, such as those involved with pathology, radiology, and the like, but are providing this care for an entire population.

The result of a bundled payment is that the providers, as a group, accept the risk for cost and outcomes. The bundle may or may not support the unit payment level they have been experiencing, and this may make for tense negotiations. It will be

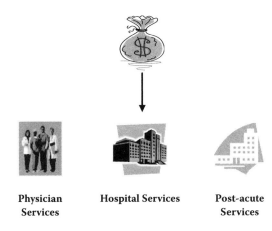

Physician   Hospital Services   Post-acute
Services   Services

Figure 6.4   Bundling diagram.

important to lay out an overall vision that reflects new realities in the marketplace. Instead of "fee-for-service" realities, these providers need to understand that these mechanisms typically have built-in quality incentives and goals. They sometimes can include only hospital payments, such as for DRGs (diagnosis related groups), but they typically include hospital and physician payments and often expand to outpatient medications, physical therapy, and postacute services. To be successful, one must redesign and optimize care, looking for efficiencies with good outcomes since the responsibility of complications and readmissions falls under this economic bundle. The reasons physicians are doing this is to increase market share and align incentives among groups to get better outcome at lower costs.

Healthcare reform calls for bundled payments (Figure 6.4) starting in February 2013; however, many pilot programs are already in place. This is a way to transfer some of the elements of performance risk to providers. So far, most of these are centered on orthopedic and cardiac procedures since they are easier to quantify. One program that is doing this is called the ACE (Acute Care Episode) bundle pilot, which looks at these surgical procedures in the Medicare population.

There are several different types of bundling models, with each moving further along the risk corridor. Classic bundle payment means paying two or more providers jointly for an episode of care. There is shared savings at the end.

- *Episode-based payments.* This model expands the bundling to include services that are delivered before and after the hospital episode of care; the length of time can be variable but often includes things such as skilled nursing facilities and home health and other outpatient entities.
- *Limited capitation.* These are fixed payments prepaid to providers who manage all care to the patient for a set period of time. This capitation can apply to specific diseases, a specific service line, or specific items of care. The model can

encompass primary care capitation, which only covers primary care services; it can be full professional capitation covering primary care and specialist care; or it can be full capitation, which covers hospital, primary care and specialty care, and all other services. Often, in this full-capitation model several things are carved out. Typical carve-outs include things that might happen out of network, organ transplants, and high-cost outliers.

To be successful in any of these models requires a team approach, often restructuring the process using Lean or other process efficiency system improvements.

Legal Limitations to Integration

There are several barriers to integration, one of which is our legal environment. Many laws were designed and made for the old medical system to try to discourage physicians from referring their patients to physicians' owned facilities. These laws in the new world of accountable care, bundling, and physician employment are antiquated and will have to be clarified before some of these new payment models can be fully employed. There are confusing antitrust policies with both Stark legislation, antikickback legislation, and the Internal Revenue Service (IRS).

The first batch of these laws involves antitrust statutes. Their purpose is to protect and ensure competition and ensure a level playing field for consumers. The U.S. Department of Justice (DOJ) and the Federal Trade Commission share authority in upholding these laws.

Traditionally, legal experts have been fairly aggressive in their approach to clinical integration. There was a general feeling that many of these physician organizations were set up as "leverage" entities to negotiate higher fees and therefore lead to less competition and a nonlevel playing field. To meet the goals of the antitrust laws, these entities have to be financially or clinically integrated in a "meaningful" way. It is only in this scenario that the ability to negotiate together for payment will not break antitrust laws.

There are many lengthy opinions on this. However, these tend not to be binding, and public entities have the right to rescind these without notice. Therefore, it is difficult to be 100% sure where the safe harbors lie.

The second major barrier to integration is the Patient Referral Act or Stark law. This law bans doctors from referring patients to facilities in which they have a financial interest. This is known as self-referral. This law requires compensation to be fixed in advance and based on the amount of effort and time worked, not based on referral volumes. This has the propensity to limit incentives for quality of care and outcome-directed payments, which are not necessarily compared to hours worked. This law needs to be reevaluated and redefined in light of clinical integration and outcome incentives.

The civil monetary law prohibits hospitals from rewarding physicians for reducing or withholding services to Medicare and Medicaid patients. This law came out of the DRG and other prospective payment systems and is administered by the OIG (Office of the Inspector General). The interpretation of this law prohibits any incentives that affect delivery of patient care. This can limit rewards for efficiency in an integrated system (depending on its interpretation). This law should not limit evidence-based medicine or medically necessary care.

The next laws to be aware of are the antikickback laws. These statutes protect patients and federal health programs from fraud and abuse. No one can willfully receive payments to influence referrals. This law has been interpreted to look carefully at the relationship between physicians and hospitals in the area of inurement.

The last governing entity involved is the IRS. Most hospitals in the United States are not for profit and therefore are exempt from federal income tax. This prevents tax-exempt institutions from being used to benefit any private individuals, including physicians. This can limit the relationships between hospitals and physicians.

All these laws together make it difficult and expensive to set up a legal entity aimed at integration of healthcare providers. According to Nick Wolter, MD, chief executive officer, Billings Clinic:

> Crucial to clinical integration is giving physicians a real involvement in decision making at the hospital. Physicians must be able to work with hospital administration to identify a shared set of goals for the enterprise—what do they want to accomplish together—and then they can together develop tactics to achieve these goals.

Figure 6.5 is a graph of different payment models, going from less integrated to more integrated. It moves from bundled payments for single episodes to bundled payments for chronic care management and eventually toward integrated PHOs, medical staff models, and finally employment with full integration. These different models offer the financial aspects of integration; however, even though aligned incentives are an extremely powerful motivator, it is necessary to have technology and process flows built to support these models.

In all of these models, there is an opportunity for misuse and overuse. Like the capitation models of the 1980s, underuse can be a concern. In all models, there must be balancing metrics, measuring outcomes both on the positive side and on the negative side. The payment model and metrics must be aligned to monitor outcomes.

All in all, this is a patient-centric approach in which the medical information follows the patient through the clinical process. Each doctor or caregiver should have access to this medical information, and embedded in this medical information should be appropriate decision support for making it "easy to do" evidence-based medicine. In this process, payment will be based on care outcomes as opposed to volume. This is the future of healthcare, but getting there will involve traveling a bumpy road.

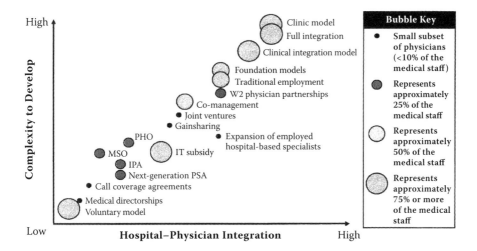

Figure 6.5   Chart integration: less to more. Consider the degree of complexity and integration of your options. Note: Foundation models refer to employment-like agreements in states where corporate practice of medicine laws prohibits direct physician employment. IT, information technology. (From Confidential & Proprietary © 2012 Sg2. Reprinted with permission.)

Information Technology

Information technology is critical for these new structures and alignments in the delivery of healthcare. This is one of the major differentiators from structures that were attempted in the 1990s. Now, we have information to impact patients' care. One of the challenges is to turn all these data into information that is actionable. This is one of the biggest challenges in healthcare. This information technology, which includes electronic medical records (EMRs) and health information exchanges (HIEs), is a critical factor that acts as an enabler for healthcare efficiency and measurable outcomes.

This should help physicians deliver and manage care for defined populations, accept payment risk, distribute savings in a shared model, and perform disease management on patient populations. In addition, it should help move us toward improved outcomes and help in predicting who will be spending healthcare dollars in the future. EMRs have also contributed to improving patient safety.

EMRs are the mainstay of these systems. These are critical for managing patient care. These hold the promise of helping to avoid duplicating tests, to practice evidence-based medicine with embedded decision support, and, importantly, to help move toward prevention and wellness by making sure all appropriate preventive and screening tests are done. In addition, EMRs should help monitor chronic diseases. This will include patients who show up to the practice on a regular basis as well as those who do not and will help move us toward population health that looks at healthcare of the population and not just healthcare at the individual patient level.

EMRs, however, are a major capital and resource expense for a practice. They require significant planning and effort and rely on significant commitment and engagement by physicians. While there are lots of controversies whether these slow the practice down or speed the practice up, these are a critical resource for tracking, trending, and quality improvement. The extent of the commitment needed to install a system is significant and must be nonnegotiable in terms of physician leadership. The preparation requires months, and the learning is ongoing, with constant and continued improvement.

An HIE is defined as a system that links many different EMR systems together. This includes linking physician practices to each other, physician practices to specialty practices, and physician practices to hospitals, pharmacies, and other healthcare providers. This is a critical piece of health information infrastructure.

One of the key tenets of this is that it takes the hospital from the central point of care and moves it into the physician community. This is sometimes complicated since hospitals typically have the capital, and often, HIE systems are either hospital or system funded or state funded through regional information exchanges.

HIEs are critical to forming medical "neighborhoods" in which the patient becomes the central point of information flow and not any one provider. The information and patient data flow from practice to practice, location to location, to make sure that the physician or other providers have all the updated information. This needs to be made possible in real time.

In addition, this lets responsible parties track the total healthcare of that individual on either an individual basis or as a population. One can track true outcomes in specific disease categories, patient categories, or others.

Information flow is critical to the future of healthcare, and while it is beyond the scope of this book to go into more detail, it is a critical piece to any type of ACO or clinical integration strategy.

Meaningful use as defined by the government employs several care processes and decision support processes that are prerequisites for a fully functioning ACO. This includes the engine behind all the necessary outcome measurements and patient tracking required for an integrated model. As you can see from Figure 6.6, the information supports different stages and is critical to an ACO.

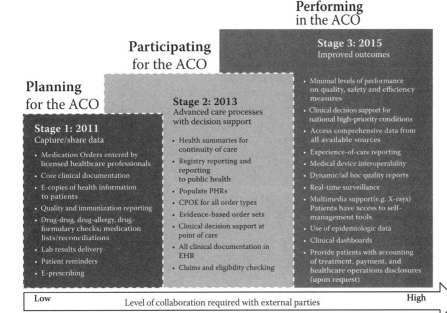

Figure 6.6 **Comparison of ACO activities with the three stages of meaningful use. CPOE, computerized physician ordered entry. (From PwC Analysis.)**

Bibliography

Allen, John, Brill, Joel, and Fogel, Ronald, *AGA statement of principles reforming the health-care system.* American Gastrological Association. April 2010. http://www.gastro.org/advocacy-regulation/legislative-issues/healthcare-reform-debate/position-statement

Allen, John, Brill, Joel, and Fogel, Ronald, *Patient centered medical home: the future of health care delivery.* American Gastrological Association. April 22, 2010. http://www.gastro.org/advocacy-regulation/legislative-issues/patient-centered-medical-home

American Gastroenterological Association. *A GIs guide to healthcare reform.* December 2010. http://www.gastro.org/advocacy-regulation/GI_Guide_to_Health-Care_Reform_Nov_2010.pdf

American Hospital Association. *Clinical integration—the key to real reform,* Trend Watch, February 2010, http://www.aha.org/research/reports/tw/10feb-clinicinteg.pdf

American Hospital Association. *Guide for clinical integration,* September 2010, http://www.aha.org/content/00-10/070417clinicalintegration.pdf

American Hospital Association. *Moving health care forward.* January 2011, http://www.aha.org/content/00-10/5barrierstoclininteg.pdf

American Urological Association. AUA health policy brief: AUA sets 2011 legislative priorities, March 2011,Washington, DC, http://www.auanet.org/eforms/hpbrief/view.cfm?i=277&a=696

Bader, Barry S. *Clinically Integrated Physician-Hospital Organizations*, Winter 2009 Great Boards, http://www.greatboards.org/newsletter/2009/Great-Boards-Winter-2009-reprint-Clinically-Integrated-PHOs.pdf

Corrigan, Karen. *The Top 10 in 2010: Ten Forces Framing Strategic Discussions for Health System Leaders.* Navvis & Company, March 2010, www.navvisandcompany.com and http://www.slideshare.net/KarenCorrigan/top-10-in-2010

Duffy, John "Hank." *A push for clinical integration*, July 2011, www.trusteemag.com and http://www.ncbi.nlm.nih.gov/pubmed/21870699

Duffy, John H., and Trent Green. *Hospital-Physician Clinical Integration.* American Hospital Association, Center for Healthcare Governance, 2010. http://www.jhdgroup.com/jhd_pdfs/JHDgroup_monograph_Hospital_Physician_Clinical_Integration.pdf.

Forecast demand by care site and disease timeline, impact of change v10.0: NIS; Pharmetrics: CMS; Sg2 Analysis. 2011. http://www.sg2.com.

Growth and performance orthopedics forecast: managing the change 2011, Sg2 Intelligence 2011, May 23, 2011. http://members.sg2.com/content-detail-standard/?ContentID=9020306193392411135

Hollingsworth, John, and Brent Hollenbeck. AUA Update Series. Vol. 29, Lesson 25. American Urological Association, 2010.

Johannessen, Wade. ABTF 2011 highlights: resetting priorities in orthopedic services, Sg2, July 20, 2011. http://members.sg2.com/content-detail-standard/?ContentID=5723192502441092808

Lloyd, Chris. HNP leading the clinical integration effort in Texas, *HNP Newslink*, Winter 2010, Memorial Hermann Health Network Providers Publication, Houston, TX, http://www.mhhnp.org/mhmd/newsletters/HNP_Newslink_Winter10.pdf

Morreale, Daniel. *Multidisciplinary clinical integration for genuine care coordination*, Health Access Solutions, www.HealthAccessSolutions.com and http://www.hasinc.com/Portals/HAS/positionpapers/genuine_care_coordination.pdf

Nielson, Eric T. *Clinical integration: a business case for quality*, October 2009 presentation, http://www.nypsystem.org/pdf/Eric_Nielsen.pdf

Sledd, Toya M. Specialists have a role in Medicare shared savings programs. American Academy of Orthopaedic Surgeons. July 2011. http://www.aaos.org/news/aaosnow/jul11/advocacy1.asp.

Sg2 Staff. *Strategies for Hospital-Physician Integration.* http://members.sg2.com/content-detail-standard/?ContentID=5419750243595782083

Taylor, Mark. Working through the frustrations of clinical integration, January 2008, *Hospitals & Health Networks.* http://www.hhnmag.com/hhnmag/jsp/articledisplay.jsp?dcrpath=HHNMAG/Article/data/01JAN2008/0801HHN_FEA_CoverStory&domain=HHNMAG

Chapter 7

Accountable Care Organizations and the Patient-Centered Medical Home

Introduction

The idea of being compensated for wellness and prevention is not a new concept and has been a noble goal for over 100 years. Some of the earlier innovations in this area occurred in the 1930s when Sidney Garfield first developed the Kaiser Permanente model of prepaid care. This model was focused on prevention and was designed to keep people out of the hospital in a gatekeeper or primary-care-oriented model.

In the 1980s, health maintenance organizations (HMOs) came into vogue. The concept of the HMOs was quite similar. Managed care companies (HMOs) were set up to focus on prevention and wellness and keep patients out of expensive medical environments by preventing events from happening. This model obviously had issues and was out of vogue by the end of the 1990s.

In 2005, Elliott Fisher of Dartmouth Institute coined the term ACO, accountable care organization, which described an integrated care delivery system that compensated providers via a shared-savings-type model (Figure 7.1).

Many critics have suggested that ACOs and HMOs are similar, and that ACOs are really "HMOs in drag." There are, however, significant differences in that ACOs do not focus on gatekeepers but advocate the development of a primary care

PHO	ACO
Insurance risk	Performance risk
Panel of patients	Population of patients
Scrum for share of revenue	Rational allocation of revenue
Charge based	Value based
Manage care leveraged	Care coordination
Episodic care focus	Patient focused
Split control and governance	Physician leadership
Do more	Do less
Intervention	Prevention
Clinical integration to achieve antitrust compliance	Clinical integration to achieve efficiencies and quality improvement

Figure 7.1 PHO versus ACO. (From Gary Scott Davis and J. Peter Rich, McDermott Will and Emory, April 14, 2010. http://www.mwe.com. Used with permission.)

patient-centered medical home (PCMH) model. They also emphasize accountability with care delivery and care decisions at the provider level rather than at a payer (or managed care) level. There are also significant linkages between quality and shared-savings incentive payments. Ultimately, Congress adapted this accountable care term in healthcare reform legislation. There is also significantly more data and information available to assist in the care for these patients than in the "HMO days."

Fisher described an ACO as a group of "… providers who are jointly held accountable for achieving measured quality improvements and reductions in the rate of spending for growth" (McClellan et al. 2010). There seem to be many different definitions of ACOs, and it is important to establish a mutually agreed definition before any further dialog on the topic.

Accountable Care Organizations

There are several different accountable care models (Figure 7.2). These are different systems of care:

1. Multispecialty groups
2. Evolution of medical staff organizational models
3. Physician-hospital organizations with clinical and financial integration

Organization	Structure	Payer	Keys for Success
Integrated systems	Physicians and hospitals under one tax ID/ organization	Insurance plans or own integrated insurance company	Aligned financial incentives, shared clinical and financial information
Multispecialty groups	Hospital may be aligned partner	Insurance plans	Alignment, data sharing, hospital partner
IPA/PHO	Must financially or clinically integrate	Insurance plans	Alignment, data sharing, hospital partner

Figure 7.2   Wide variety of ACO models.

4. Independent physician organizations or independent practice association (IPA) type models
5. Health plan and provider collaborative organizations or networks

Each of these models offers advantages and disadvantages in trying to vertically and horizontally integrate the care process. These models also offer different opportunities in terms of sharing clinical data, whether it would be from the claim side (if an insurer is involved) or through linking strategies of different providers and provider organizations.

Regardless of different structures, there are typical characteristics that are part of an ACO. These include

- Collaboration
- Care management policies that support population-based health (Figure 7.3)
- Patient-centered practices that engage the patient
- EMRs (electronic medical records) or health information technology (IT) that enable utilization of electronic information
- A focus on service and patient excellence
- A shared-savings model with mechanisms to share savings based on quality and patient experience
- A "care" orientation

There has been significant discussion on the startup cost to develop an ACO. The Centers for Medicare and Medicaid Services (CMS) estimated the cost as approximately $1.7 million per ACO based on a 2008 Government Accounting Office (GAO) study. However, several other demonstration pilots have suggested considerably less.

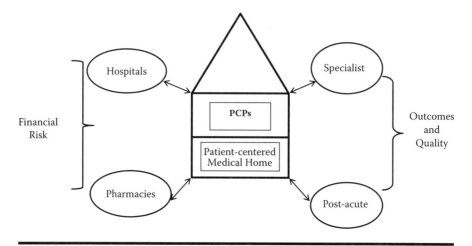

Figure 7.3 Accountable care organization accountability for health. PCP, primary care provider.

It is important to distinguish that while ACO is a term that often is related to Medicare's definition of an ACO, it is really more of a concept than a definition. The Medicare definition was first introduced on March 31, 2011, with a recent amendment of those definitions. It is beyond the scope of this book to discuss the specific definitions of a CMS ACO since these may change over time. Suffice it to say that there is much published information on Medicare's definition that includes the exact nature of risk sharing, metrics, and exact way that patients will be attributed.

The Medicare CMS ACO projects are just getting under way and more definitions will certainly be forthcoming. There are also many commercial ACOs that are already in pilot stages and continue to be developed (Figure 7.4). In 2005, CMS contracted with 10 large multispecialty groups to create a Medicare physician group practice as a demonstration project to prove that these models could save up to $38 million in Medicare costs (Inglehart, 2011).

The National Committee for Quality Assurance (NCQA) is starting to develop an accreditation process and has proposed seven domains to evaluate an ACO:

- Structure and operations
- Access to providers
- Patient-centered primary care
- Care management
- Care coordination and transition
- Patient rights and responsibilities
- Performing, reporting, and quality

These criteria mimic the managed care NCQA accreditation process.

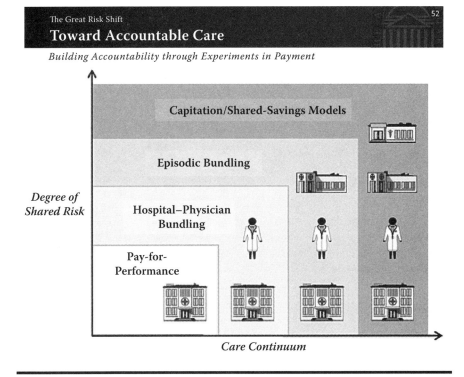

Figure 7.4 Toward accountable care: building accountability through experiments in payment. (© 2010 The Advisory Board Company. All rights reserved. Reprinted with permission.)

One of the critical characteristics is care management. This includes a primary-care-focused collaboration and coordination of care across the entire care continuum. The focus is on evidence-based care, supported by IT, which transitions information to each provider in the care process so that tests are not repeated and the appropriate diagnosis is made quickly. Since information is available to each provider whether it is the hospital, outpatient, pharmacy, or physician's office, it requires a significant infrastructure investment (Figure 7.5).

The next requirement is a patient-centered focus. The PCMH concept is an ideal vehicle as an underpinning for an accountable care structure. There must also be significant financial infrastructure so that the different payment models and mechanisms can be managed and savings can be calculated, analyzed, and shared on an equitable basis. Last, an appropriate culture shift to include wellness, prevention, and "well care" instead of "sick care" must be undertaken. This requires leadership on the physician's side.

It is also critical that the financial arrangements be tracked carefully since there must be a division of money based on a predetermined formula. This requires a sophisticated accounting system.

		Health Care Providers Included		Examples of Cost Reduction Opportunities
Level 4 ACO		Public Health		Coordinated Health and Social
		Safety-Net Clinics		Services Support
	Level 3 ACO	Hospitals		Improved Management of
		Other Specialists		Complex Patients
		Level 2 ACO Major Specialists (cardiology, orthopedics, etc)		Improved Outcomes and Efficiency for Major Specialities
		Level 1 ACO Primary Care Practice	Primary Care Practice	Reduction in Preventable ED Visits and Admissions
		Primary Care Practice	Primary Care Practice	Appropriate Use of Testing/Referral
		Primary Care Practice	Primary Care Practice	Prevention and Early Diagnosis

Figure 7.5   Which models can we use? (From Miller HD, *How to Create Accountable Care Organizations*. Pittsburgh, PA: Center for Healthcare Quality and Payment Reform, February 2010, Sg2. With permission.)

One particular challenge in this new structure is patient engagement. This has been a frustration of healthcare practitioners for many years in that the patient will not participate in his or her care with healthcare decision making, healthy behavior, or compliance with medical therapies (or medications). This model emphasizes patient involvement in both decision making and patient understanding of personal healthcare issues. This requires a team approach to care be adopted by surgeons, physicians, nurses, and healthcare administrators. One critical piece of infrastructure is a patient's (IT) portal so patients can communicate directly with the providers via e-mail to obtain appropriate medical information through e-services, appointment scheduling, prescription ordering, and other communications. This has been shown to generate increased patient satisfaction.

Telemedicine and e-health are important developments, and e-visits and monitoring through electronic means can be a great way to affect more efficient care. One of the challenges of our current system is it often does not pay for e-visits. In a new ACO model, if it is the most effective and efficient way care can be provided, it should be compensated.

Another critical piece of an ACO must be data aggregation, collection, and analysis. Most ACOs, including the CMS ACO project, have significant quality, cost, and utilization metrics that must be measured and reported. A patient's satisfaction is a also critical metric. This leads to another key piece of an ACO: population health management (i.e., looking at populations of health rather than just an individual patient from the practice level). This is a new way of thinking for most providers.

An ounce of prevention is worth the pound of cure—and costs a lot less.

(Unknown source)

The infrastructure must be adequate to manage the financial reimbursement models. These models can have either one-sided risk or two-sided risk. The one-sided risk is usually upside. In other words, the physician or practice (or ACO) cannot lose money but shares the gains. In the two-sided risk model, the practices can both gain and lose money depending on how efficient the care is; however, the gain is more significant in this model since there is downside risk. To be successful, there must be significant infrastructure inside the practice to evaluate medical necessity, preauthorization, and evidence-based care.

ACOs will change financial incentives significantly since physicians will be doing more to coordinate care and focus on prevention and wellness. The current health system, which rewards volume of care versus clinical outcomes, is unsustainable, and must evolve into a performance-based system. Hospitals, which traditionally hire doctors who are "superstars," will change their focus instead on hiring doctors who can work in a team environment focusing on patient care. Accountability will be a significant "disruptive technology" in healthcare if it is done properly. Traditionally, ACOs became synonymous with Medicare shared-savings/pioneer programs; however, this is not accurate. ACOs are equally prevalent in the commercial and (eventually) Medicaid world, where the definitions will be less rigid. The objective of integration will not be reduction in overhead or use of on-call sharing, but true creation of an enterprise that focuses on wellness and prevention rather than a sickness-based system. Capitation has not worked well in a fragmented system but has worked well in an integrated system, as the Kaiser-like models.

Care will shift from episodic acute care treatment to wellness and prevention (keeping the patients out of the hospital). This needs to include patient engagement, chronic disease management, predictive modeling, population-based health, and others. Healthcare providers will need to be in the "business of health" and not in the business of "managing sick" patients. This is where value really gets created in healthcare, and innovation can proceed based on what is best for the patient, not the economics and reimbursement models that are perverse.

One important change is in the area of risk. Risk has traditionally been under the singular territory of insurance companies, which have conducted actuarial analysis and structured risk-based agreements using a fee-for-service model. In the future, risk will be transitioned to the point of care. This must be carefully balanced since prior experience with risk (i.e., capitation) was not consistently effective. Risk must be shared with some of the risk being held, initially, by the insurers and some shifted to the provider, who is in the best position to control the balance among cost, utilization, and quality.

There are three areas of major savings in an accountability-type model. The first areas of opportunity are the "low-hanging fruit." These include:

1. Preventable events, which include duplicative testing, non-evidence-based medical procedures
2. Preventable complications, which include postoperative infections, falls, deep venous thrombosis
3. Preventable readmission, which indicates returns to the hospital could have been avoided with a careful transition process to the outpatient environment
4. Preventable admissions, which can be caused by patients not seeking care sooner and lack of close outpatient follow-up
5. Preventable ancillary services
6. Preventable emergency room visits by providing access for nonurgent care in a safe, less-expensive outpatient environment

The second-tier opportunities are based on chronic illness management. This includes chronic diseases that are prevalent, especially as a patient becomes older, such as diabetes, hypertension, congestive heart failure, asthma, and cancers. In addition, reduction of obesity rates and other preventive risks presents an opportunity.

The last tier of opportunities is medical system management. Physicians need to start focusing on transitions of care across the outpatient environment (Figure 7.6). This includes hospitalist programs, postdischarge care management, appropriate hospice management, and telehealth/e-visits. It also may include complex case management.

 It is clear that ACOs are not one thing but more of a "concept of design," including transitions of care, preventable care, and the "triple aim." The triple aim includes improving the health of the population, enhancing the patient experience of care, and reducing or at least controlling the cost of care. This focus requires a patient-centered approach often exemplified by the PCMH model.

Patient-Centered Medical Home

Many medical experts believe that a foundation of future accountable care (ACO) models will be the PCMH. This is an old concept that is becoming new again with primary care physicians taking ownership, control, and coordination of a patient's care.

One of the big challenges in this arena is the lack of a firm, consistent definition (Figure 7.7) of what a PCMH is. Most understand that it is about care coordination, population health, availability of same-day appointments, and access to care. There is no clear definition at this point. You can see from Figure 7.8, with components combined from various medical societies, that there are many components of PCMH that define it.

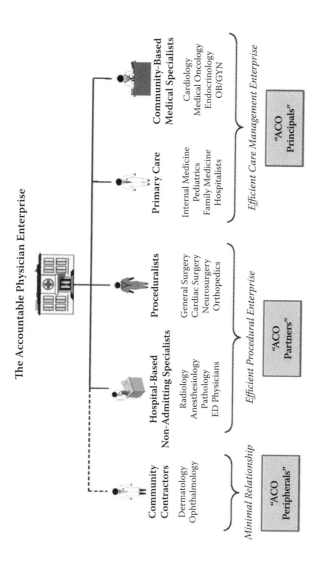

Figure 7.6 Physicians segment according to role in ACO. (From © 2010 The Advisory Board Company. All rights reserved. Reprinted with permission.)

Medical Home

American Academy of Pediatrics definition: "A medical home is a community-based primary care setting that integrates quality and evidence-based standards in providing and coordinating family-centered health promotion in wellness, acute and chronic condition management."

Figure 7.7 Definition of medical home according to the American Academy of Pediatrics. (From Starfield, B., and L. Shi. The medical home, access to care, and insurance: a review of evidence. *Pediatrics* 2004; 113:1493–1498.)

Many hope that the medical home concept (Figure 7.9) will reinvigorate primary care, leading to more physicians choosing this as a specialty. This concept initially started with a national demonstration project in 2006, although it was actually coined earlier in a book published by the American Academy of Pediatrics in 1967 and then again in 2004 when the American Academy of Family Physicians suggested that every American should have a "medical home."

In June 2006, the demonstration project started with two groups of randomized physician groups: facilitated intervention and self-directed care. It included more than 50 individual components. It was discovered that discrete improvements could be done fairly simply, yet transforming the whole practice was much more difficult, particularly in smaller practices. The team-based approach to care was also a big challenge, and many of the small practices had trouble meeting this requirement. One controversy is whether this team-based concept has to be led by a physician or can be led by a nurse practitioner, physician assistant, or registered nurse.

Another concept in the medical home model is the importance of an IT infrastructure. This typically includes an EMR to allow the practice to focus on population-based healthcare. It also includes an HIE (health insurance exchange) strategy so that multiple EMRs can communicate with each other and share information to efficiently manage the patient's care.

These principles are becoming more codified as accrediting bodies for PCMHs are adapting criteria. The most common is the NCQA. The NCQA PCMH Recognition Program started in 2008 and has evolved. Other accrediting bodies, such as the Joint Commission on Accreditation of Healthcare Organizations (JCAHO) and Utilization Review Accreditation Committee (URAC), are developing PCMH accreditation programs. There are also many consultants who are stepping up to assist practices in shaping goals and achieving accreditation.

There is still some controversy about the financial and clinical benefits of PCMHs. There are multiple studies that have been conducted, with some conflicting results. One study by the NCQA found no increase in practice expenses, while others have shown significant cost to the practice for practice development. Some studies have shown up to a 26% dividend in becoming a medical home, but others

A continuous relationship with a personal physician coordinating care for both wellness and illness

- Mindful clinician-patient communication: trust, respect, shared decision making
- Patient engagement
- Provider/patient partnership
- Culturally sensitive care
- Continuous relationship
- Whole-person care

Access to Care and Information	Practice Management	Practice-Based Services	Practice-Based Team Care
Same-day appointments	Disciplined financial management	Comprehensive care/chronic conditions	Provider leadership
After-hours access coverage	Revenue enhancement	Prevention screening and services	Shared mission and vision
Accessible patient/lab information	Cost-benefit decision making	Surgical procedures	Effective communication
Online patient services	Optimized coding/billing	Ancillary therapeutic/ support services	Task designation by skill set
E-visits	Personnel/ human resources management	Ancillary diagnostic services	Nurse practitioner/ physician assistant
Group visits	Facilities management		Patient participation
Culturally sensitive care	Optimized office design		Family involvement options
	Change management		

continued

Figure 7.8 Patient-centered medical home concepts. (Adapted from *Joint Principals or PCMH and Guidelines* released by AAFP, AAP, ACP, AOA in 2007.)

Care Coordination	Care Management	Health Information Technology	Quality and Safety
Community-based resources	Population management	Electronic medical record	Evidence-based best practices
Collaborative relationships	Wellness promotion	Electronic orders and reporting	Medication management
Emergency room	Disease prevention	E-prescribing	Patient satisfaction feedback
Hospital care	Chronic disease management	Evidence-based decision support	Clinical outcomes analysis
Maternity care	Patient engagement and education	Population management registry	Quality improvement
Specialist care	Leverages automated technologies	Practice Web site	Risk management
Pharmacy		Patient portal	Regulatory compliance
Physical therapy			
Case management			
Care transition			

Figure 7.8 (continued)

have not. One of the key concepts in this medical home initiative is how physicians will be paid for this service. There are several options available, including

1. An increase in fee-for-service payments for practices that are accredited
2. Reimbursement of health professionals for specific activities based on time spent
3. Payment of a lump sum to a practice or a per member per month amount on top of their fee-per-service payment
4. A capitated payment for services to cover all medical costs
5. Payment of a bonus for targeted quality and outcomes metrics (and possibly utilization metrics)
6. Payment to physicians for a share of any savings that are generated relative to prior historical costs (Figure 7.10).

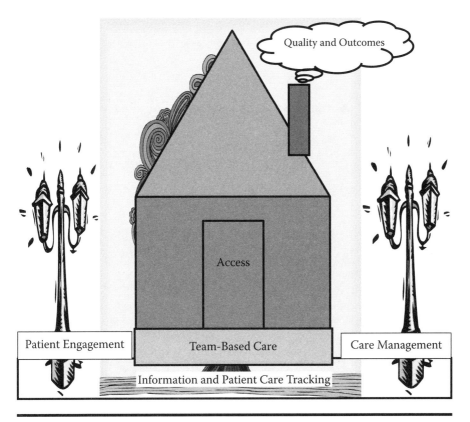

Figure 7.9   Patient-centered medical home as a hub.

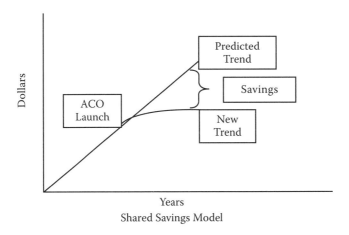

Figure 7.10   Healthcare costs according to the shared savings model.

Most current models use a combination of these payment mechanisms. All in all, there has to be revenue to compensate for the additional time and effort involved in becoming a PCMH.

How Doctors Want to Be Paid for Providing a Medical Home

Four physician societies issued joint principles they hoped would underlie any new medical home payment model (Figure 7.11).

One other extension of the medical home concept is evolving the "home" into a healthcare neighborhood (Figure 7.12). This involves much more than just the primary care aspect of a medical practice and integrates the entire healthcare experience across the vertical and horizontal clinical continuums. This shifts the PCMH into an ACO. Many believe that this basic infrastructure of a medical home is critical to an accountability project with primary care coordination and population health management.

There is implicit linkage in the medical home concept in the ACO language in the healthcare reform bill. It is easier to see the PCMH as a new alignment strategy that may prove to have the critical infrastructure needed to move toward greater transformation and alignment.

• Reflect the value of care management work that falls outside the face-to-face visit.
• Pay for care coordination within a practice and between providers.
• Support adoption and use of health IT for quality improvement.
• Support the provision of e-mail and telephone consultation.
• Recognize the value of remote monitoring of clinical data using technology.
• Maintain payment levels for face-to-face visits, despite the new payments listed above.
• Recognize case mix differences in the patient populations served by practices.
• Allow medical homes to share in savings from reduced hospitalizations generated by their active management of their patients' care.
• Allow for quality bonus payments for achieving measurable and continuous quality improvements.

Figure 7.11 Joint principles for the patient-centered medical home concept. (From summary of *Joint Principles of the PC MH* released by the AAFP, AAP, ACP, and AOA in 2007.)

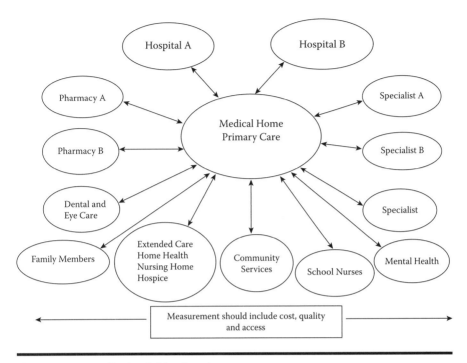

Figure 7.12   Medical neighborhood.

Bibliography

Aderholdt, Betsy and Jeff Lockridge, Partnering with doctors through co-management, *Health Progress*, July–August 2011, www.chausa.org/; http://www.google.com/ url?sa= t&rct=j&q=partnering%20with%20doctors%20through%20comanagement%E2%80 %9D%2C%20betsy%20aderholdt%20and%20jeff%20lockridge%2C%20 health%20progress&source=web&cd=1&sqi=2&ved=0CEQQFjAA&url=http%3A %2F%2Fwww.chausa.org%2Fworkarea%2FDownloadAsset.aspx%3Fid%3D429496 8919&ei=KI0qUP6VNWywHE84GYCQ&usg=AFQjCNH1fUeaWqFx6XDVgCKI 3DQAaasi5g&cad=rjt

American Hospital Association. *Moving health care forward*, January 2011, http://www.aha.org/ content/00-10/5barrierstoclininteg.pdf

Arvantes, James. Geisinger Health System reports that PCMH model improves quality, lowers costs, May 26, 2010, www.aafp.org and http://www.aafp.org/online/en/home/ publications/news/news-now/practice-management/20100526geisinger.html

Barrett, Tricia Marine, Greg Carlson, Waco Hoover, Craig Samitt, Kashitij Savena, Ben Wilson, Eleanor Burnon, and Virginia Traweek. Accountable care organizations: 10 things you need to know about accountable care. Institute for Health Technology Transformation. October 21, 2011. http://www.ihealthtran.com/pdf/iHT2ACOReport.pdf

Berkson, Doug. Exploring the medical home, expanding to the medical neighborhood (utilizing unwarranted variation as a framework), Spring Managed Care Forum, Orlando, FL, April 22, 2010. http://www.healthdialog.com/Utility/News/Events- AndWebcasts/10-04-22/NAMCP_Spring_Managed_Care_Forum

Blue Cross Blue Shield of Hawaii. *HMSA patient-centered medical home*, http://www.hmsa.com/providers/assets/HMSA_PCMHProgramGuide.pdf, 2012

Boland, Peter, Phil Polakoff, and Ted Schwab, Accountable care organizations hold promise, but will they achieve cost and quality targets? *Managed Care*, October 2010. http://www.managedcaremag.com/archives/1010/1010.ACOs.html

Cohen, Robert. *Clinical co-management summary*, Kutak Rock LLP, http://www.kutakrock.com/publications/healthcare/MEMO_CCMS.pdf

Corrigan, Karen. *The Top 10 in 2010: ten forces framing strategic discussions for health system leaders*, Navvis & Company, March 2010. http://www.slideshare.net/KarenCorrigan/top-10-in-2010

Forecast demand by care site and disease timeline, impact of change v10.0: NIS; Pharmetrics: CMS; Sg2 Analysis. 2011. http://www.sg2.com.

Karamchedu, Murali, Sam Muppalla, and Robert Capobianco, Moving beyond Medicare's ACOs to accountable care, *American Health & Drug Benefits*, July/August 2011, 4(4): 204–206. http://www.ahdbonline.com/article/moving-beyond-medicare%E2%80%99s-acos-accountable-care

Kennedy, Kelly. Accountable care groups gain acceptance. *USA Today*, July 24, 2011. http://www.usatoday.com/NEWS/usaedition/2011-07-25-accountable21_ST_U.htm

Mauer, Barbara J. National overview: behavioral health primary care integration and the person-centered healthcare home, National Council for Community Behavioral Healthcare, January 12, 2009. http://www.healthleadersmedia.com/content/MAG-270678/Making-Margin-with-the-Medical-Home.html

McClellan, Mark and Elliott Fisher, *Structuring outcomes–based payments*, Accountable Care Organization Learning Network, The Brookings Institution, Washington, DC. https://xteam.brookings.edu/bdacoln/Documents/ACO%20Toolkit%20January%202011.pdf

McLaughlin, Robert. The accountable care organization: partnering to deliver value, www.Cigna.com. http://www.hc21.org/files/McLaughlin%202011.pdf

Medical homes in 2011: one-third to join an accountable care organization, April 2011 survey results. http://www.hin.com/library/registerpcmh2011.html

Miller, H.D. *How to Create Accountable Care Organizations.* Pittsburgh, PA: Center for Healthcare Quality and Payment Reform, February 2010, Sg2

Miller, Harold D. Transitioning to accountable care, Center for Healthcare Quality & Payment Reform, Pittsburgh, PA. http://www.chqpr.org/downloads/Transitioningto-AccountableCare.pdf

Minich-Ourshadi, Karen. Making margin with the medical home, September 2011, http://www.healthleadersmedia.com/content/MAG-270678/Making-Margin-with-the-Medical-Home.html

Mirvis, David M. "Accountable care organizations: a real change, maybe", *Tennessee Medicine*, www.tnmed.org, October 2011. http://www.omagdigital.com/display_article.php?id=853234

Morreale, Daniel. *Multidisciplinary clinical integration for genuine care coordination*, Health Access Solutions, www.HealthAccessSolutions.com/ http://www.hasinc.com/Portals/HAS/positionpapers/genuine_care_coordination.pdf

Nutting, P., B. Crabtree, W. Miller et al. Transforming physician practices to patient-centered medical homes: lessons from the national demonstration project. 2011. *Health Affairs*, 30(3):439–445.

Putting It All Together. Quality Improvement and Your Practice. http://www.doctorsadvocate. org/wp-content/uploads/2011/05/DoctorsDigest_PuttingItTogether.pdf

Sg2 Staff. *Strategies for hospital–physician integration,* www.sg2.com/ http://members.sg2.com/ content-detail-standard/?ContentID=5419750243595782083

Starfield, B., and L. Shi. The medical home, access to care, and insurance: a review of evidence. *Pediatrics,* 113: 1493–1498 (2004).

Sutariya, Bharat, and Clay Patterson. Accountable for health. Cerner Corporation. 2010. http://www.cerner.com.

Chapter 8

Assessing Your Current Alignment Strategy

To assess the relevance of your current physician alignment strategy, an initial place to start would be with the question of whether an explicit strategy currently exists. Many organizations feel compelled to make decisions to solve a problem with one or more physicians quickly, but they often do this in a strategic vacuum. This is quite common even in individual hospitals that are part of systems. It can appear that each facility has a different alignment strategy. In fact, it may actually be appropriate for each facility to choose to implement different initiatives.

Every facility or system has a physician alignment strategy. It is either explicit or implicit. In this chapter, we assist in determining the best fit between your alignment strategy and the environment that you face. The environment can be impacted by factors such as the local economic conditions, the strategies of your competitors, your current market position, and both current and projected service line development. Assessing your current strengths, weaknesses, threats, and opportunities pertaining to physician relationships is an important starting point in determining the efficacy of your current strategy.

To be relevant and impactful, your alignment strategy should reflect what you know about your organization, your market, and often your competitors. A comprehensive physician alignment strategy should complement and flow from your strategic plan, not refute it. If your current enterprise strategy in no way emphasizes physician relationships, your first order might be to assess how badly operations would be disrupted if you do not have a comprehensive and well-timed physician alignment strategy. It will be "heavy lifting" to use an alignment plan to change corporate understanding and culture.

Assuming that you have determined that a strong base of physicians who are tightly aligned with your hospital is or will be important to your long-term success, the alignment plan must anticipate correct tactics, timing, and necessary resources to implement the plan successfully.

In the continuum of alignment tactics expressed in this book, there are factors to consider that will help you determine which tactics to employ. In many ways, you know the culture of your organization and your organizational readiness for these strategies. As the options are evaluated, it will be important to remember that someone, most likely in planning or finance, will need to understand the return on investment (ROI) these strategies will yield. This is not just about money—the resources used to implement an alignment strategy will include time, political capital, and relationship building (and maintenance).

The economic factors and drivers operating in healthcare today generally point to an alignment strategy that must keep advancing the organization further down the continuum, toward a more highly integrated relationship with physicians. It is not necessary that every point on the alignment continuum be explored and implemented. However, assessing which offers the best return and best fits in your environment and culture will be crucial.

Ensuring such a review is well grounded and focused could be accomplished in several ways. For the purpose of this analysis, we are choosing to review issues based on internal and external factors. The internal factors that would determine the best fit for an alignment strategy would likely begin with the medical staff. If the hospital's geography, corporate culture, and past physician relationships have led to a medical staff who are cohesive and already highly aligned, then that offers a good foundation to move toward a more sophisticated model. If, however, the voluntary medical staff equally splits their time and loyalty among one or more additional facilities, more organizational work may be required to further educate the medical staff about the current and future state of healthcare and the higher level of integration that will be essential for future success. More than likely, varying levels of loyalty and exclusivity exist within each specialty. An additional internal factor to consider involves identifying the most important service lines to the hospital and measuring alignment potential with a resolve toward protecting existing market share and profitability. If we suspect bundled payments are coming our way in service lines that are or will be very important to our financial future, developing alignment efforts in these categories would be a high priority.

Another internal factor would be the level to which the hospital has the management talent and resources to implement simultaneous tactics that improve alignment. In many cases, as hospitals divested more advanced alignment tactics in the past, they also reemphasized bread-and-butter hospital management talent as opposed to those with advanced skills in managing the ambulatory continuum of care. It may be necessary to add to the hospital's clinical and administrative talent those who have experience in physician joint ventures or practice management. It may also be necessary to acquire consulting or managerial talent to assist in assessing readiness for certain strategies, such as development of an accountable care organization (ACO) or physician employment. As an entity moves up the continuum of plans to improve alignment, it is moving into territory where more advanced models will require experience and expertise that may be beyond that offered by existing leadership. If the strategy you choose involves business models of employment, you are likely to find the need to recruit new management talent that has had experience growing and operating physician practices. The same can be said for ACO development as this venture will require someone in leadership who has experience in managed care, cost, and outcomes in a risk environment such as a health maintenance organization (HMO) or capitated physician group. Unfortunately, these individuals do not exist in great number and are likely geographically concentrated.

If the medical staff itself does not yet understand the capabilities necessary to thrive in the future economic models, a comprehensive educational effort will be necessary to bring the medical staff "up to speed." If you do not, developments that appear aggressive or rapid could make the staff uneasy. The future models will be transformational, and the attributes of success in a capitated world are far different from those you would make in the fee-for-service world. The definition of success is being upended by these changes. In any case, a thorough review of the internal factors that affect the success of alignment activities will help determine needs and timing for your activities and any foundation work that may precede implementation.

One factor you may face is the fatigue of those who "rode on this merry-go-round before." Depending on the history of the hospital and previous strategies that may have been employed 10 to 15 years ago, you may encounter the crowd with the attitude of "we tried that before and it didn't work." These folks have a point that must be acknowledged even as we work hard to ensure we do not repeat the same mistakes. To calm their fears, it may be appropriate to invite these leaders to be involved in development committees that support your change. For these individuals, it will be important to stress the differences between the economic factors, tactics, and future demands as they exist today versus the past. Rightly acknowledging the skeptics and bringing them into the fold to help ensure that those same mistakes are not made can be an important factor in building credibility.

Another important internal factor that bears discussion is the hospital's financial performance and balance sheet. To the extent that it is positive and perhaps strong, it will be that much more important to educate the staff and medical staff about upcoming changes that could threaten stability. There may be push back to tinkering with "what's working." It will be important to stress that the shift toward fixed global payments will undermine existing success factors in a way that sends everybody back to the drawing board to rethink economics of the plan.

Key Strategic Considerations
Internal
• Level of cohesion in medical staff
• Existing key service lines
• Hospital management talent
• Historical alignment position
• Strength of facility balance sheet
External
• Competition's alignment plans
• Physician readiness
• Competitive strength of facility
• Level of primary care shortage
• Employer position
• Payer needs and expectations

Another vantage point from which to assess your current and potential alignment strategies involves looking externally at those factors that will have an impact on success. Such external factors will include the local healthcare environment, your competition's efforts, and your competitive position with both payer and employer expectations. The local healthcare environment will have an impact on the strategies you employ based on the readiness of the community as a whole for change and disruption. If physicians in your community are under duress, which is common in many communities, they may be clamoring for the development of employed and aligned models. They may actually be more ready for alignment tactics than the facility or system. The greater the burden of indigent patients on community physicians, the more likely that the community will be facing economic challenges that will force alignment at a faster pace.

If, as a facility, you are acting from a dominant competitive position and are not yet enjoying a highly aligned relationship with physicians, your reasons to advance along the continuum will be highly defensive and implemented with a mind-set to maintain dominance. If you are acting from a position where you do not enjoy dominance, your reasoning will be more about offensive moves to help change that dynamic. Keep in mind that no one can predict the pace of reimbursement reform, but it could provide a significant impetus to advance the strategy sooner as opposed to later. With respect to competitive forces, alignment efforts will be driven by the desire to grow or ensure market share in profitable specialties as well as implement initiatives to lower cost in anticipation of lower future reimbursement. Ignoring the development efforts of the competition will be dangerous. Numerous examples exist since 2005 of a hospital that lost its dominance in a specialty service line because a competitor "beat it to the punch" in alignment efforts. It will be important to assess where your competition is in developing an alignment plan and gauge their pace and tactics as you develop your plan. It will not be necessary to create an identical plan or equally timed plan, but it will be important to assess the risks of the pace you have chosen and be ready to pick up the pace if necessary.

It is important that you not ignore the primary care community in this review. The prevalence or lack of primary care differs from community to community, and some alignment models depend on an adequate supply to implement new models of care. Review carefully what your competitor's capacity and readiness are to develop a strongly aligned primary care provider base. It is from that primary care base that the facility would have the strength to develop a highly aligned specialty physician group. Key indicators of such readiness would include capital to purchase practices, talent to manage the enterprise, infrastructure on which to manage practices, and the ability to bill and collect for physician practices.

Previous chapters have outlined the changing philosophies of governmental payers, including the likelihood that increased focus and risk will be placed on outcomes and population health. If those in the employer community feel they are sharing an unfair burden of the cost of care to cover indigent patients or have seen explosive growth in duplicative service lines, they are likely to conclude that they will benefit from alignment efforts, especially those that wring costs out of the system. Employers are wary of shifting even more cost to employees, and this promotes discussion and planning for a restructured delivery system and increased readiness for change. It is wise to keep the dialogue with the payers open. They are likely to challenge you to move at a more rapid pace to achieve savings and better outcomes from successful alignment.

After evaluating internal and external factors that will have an impact on your plan and assessing readiness for movement along the continuum, you will need to choose the strategies that are best for your situation. In general, they will be categorized as less-complex and more-complex initiatives. The less-complex tactics to improve alignment involve developing an independent practice association (IPA) or physician hospital organization (PHO) relationship with key segments of your medical staff. For the IPA or PHO, you could offer MSO (medical service organization) services and information technology (IT) assistance that could help them achieve meaningful use under recent IT legislation. While these tactics have no guarantee of increasing admissions or growing market share among key service lines, they could provide the foundation for the relationship to grow more integrated as the parties grow in understanding and trust of one another. In terms of preparing for risk, the PHO or IPA could serve as the organization through which bundled payments could be administered and the funds flow to participating providers. A more advanced form of joint venture would be a clinical co-management arrangement. Focused on efficiency and care improvement, these arrangements would be an excellent strategy to garner physician attention to the things that matter: quality, cost, and volume. A key aspect of these strategies is that they leave each business entity intact and do not represent fundamental integration of business units into the enterprise. A careful review, usually by an outside expert, should provide details on whether there was enough potential savings to fund such alignment initiatives.

In contrast, more complex strategies generate a fundamental change in ownership and genuine enterprise thinking that has eluded planners in the past. These tactics would include traditional employment relationships, foundation models, professional service agreements, and development of an ACO. If one viewed the former tactics as dating, these involve full-blown matrimony. As such, they take longer to implement and offer far more finality in their structure; consequently, they are a far stronger alignment tactic. Just because they are more final does not mean your organization must progress through the tactics at a slow pace. In fact, some organizations may bypass lesser forms of alignment in favor of more advanced tactics precisely because the physicians and hospital see no benefit from less-integrative strategies. Reasons for this would include radical competitive changes, economic factors in the community, and a generally strong bond between key medical staff members and the facility. If such is the case and you advance quickly to a higher form of alignment, key issues would be capital requirements and acquiring the infrastructure to support this development. At all times, it will be important to thoroughly articulate in your planning the reasons you are doing this and what your financial expectations are for this venture. If your development is phased based on a service line or specialty, it will be important that the remainder of the medical staff be educated regarding the underlying economic forces driving the change and the pace of the expected change. Otherwise, other motives might be attached to your efforts. Be aware that large and more powerful groups may view the effort as upsetting the balance of power, and they may be tentative in supporting what may seem reasonable to others. Transparency with the key medical staff about your alignment strategy will be key to maintaining support within the medical staff and minimizing negative political impact for hospital leadership.

Less Complex Alignment Tactics
• IPA/PHO creation
• IT assistance
More Complex Tactics
• Employment/PSA (physician service agreement) arrangements
• Clinical co-management
• ACO development

Once developed, key elements of the alignment plan could become the subject of a board retreat, medical staff leadership retreats, and other venues that foster understanding and support. While it will be important to keep some proprietary details private in these presentations, setting out the alignment philosophy with the medical staff will help create a healthier expectation as the plan evolves over time. As these developments demand capital and may redesign referral patterns and growth opportunities, the medical staff could witness big changes in the decisions made by the facility. Some of these decisions may look radical compared to previous initiatives. For this reason, sounding the bell that you have "turned the corner" on this strategy will be helpful in creating an environment that expects and even supports change. As competitive forces chip away at planning assumptions, periodic revisiting of these will be important to retain relevance to the current business and competitive environment. In addition, these course corrections will assist you in gaining credibility with facility staff, medical staff, and other interested stakeholders.

Chapter 9

Examples of Systems Strategic Alignment Initiatives

Methodist Le Bonheur Healthcare

William Breen, Jr.

A typical Southern city challenged by the factors that make it difficult to improve population health would be Memphis, Tennessee. Located on the Mississippi River at the nexus of three states (Tennessee, Mississippi, and Arkansas), Memphis is challenged by poverty, barriers to access, and chronic shortages of primary care. Methodist Le Bonheur Healthcare (MLH) represents the largest system in the metro area (based on licensed hospital beds) and geographic points. MLH has embraced its mission orientation and partnered closely with the faith community through its recently created Congregational Health Network (CHN). Through CHN, health navigators have been created in health communities, and to date, CHN has grown to include over 500 churches in the region.

The goal of the CHN is to connect the access points between MLH and those it serves to improve patient experience, health outcomes, and overall population health working through religious communities.

MLH currently enjoys an A rating from financial rating agencies and has a strong balance sheet. In 2012, MLH operated five adult hospitals and was building a sixth hospital in the growing suburb of Olive Branch, Mississippi. In addition, MLH operates Le Bonheur Children's Hospital, a 235-bed facility nationally recognized for cardiac, neurological, and orthopedic care for children. In addition, Le Bonheur Children's Hospital is a partner with St. Jude Children's Research Hospital.

In most healthcare trends, Memphis lags behind other parts of the United States. One example of this is development of employed medical groups. This trend began in early 2010 in the Memphis market, a full decade behind other communities. Another factor setting Memphis apart from most other communities is the fact that nearly all commercially insured members are steered toward either MLH or its competitor, Baptist Memorial Health Care. Currently, MLH enjoys preferred network status with Cigna Healthcare, United Healthcare, and Blue Cross Blue Shield of Tennessee. This commanding managed care lead is a factor that influences many other aspects of strategy and competition.

In the arena of employment/professional service agreements, Methodist has strong partners in cardiology, cardiovascular surgery, oncology, and primary care. These specialties have been a focus for MLH since 2010. In addition, as the main teaching hospital for the University of Tennessee School of Medicine, MLH has created adult and pediatric practice plans to support the clinical practice of the university's physicians serving these populations. In total, MLH has nearly 310 highly aligned employed physicians in a community of approximately 2000 physicians. Together with its competitors, hospitals were employed or highly aligned with approximately 30% of primary care physicians and 20% of area specialties as of mid-2012.

Co-owned by MLH and key physician partners, the physician hospital organization (PHO) Health Choice began developing the concept of an accountable care organization (ACO) with a key insurer partner, Cigna Healthcare, in 2009. As the largest insurer in the region with 250,000 covered lives, Cigna was interested in developing a pilot in Memphis that was different from its prior ACO pilots. In this model, the patients are treated by numerous nonaligned primary care providers (PCPs) organized around the PHO. As of mid-2012, there were approximately 18,000 members in the pilot being served by care coordinators, who were registered nurses imbedded in seven practices around the community. The financial and clinical results of the pilot are being compared to previous trends experienced for their patients prior to these interventions. Both Cigna and Health Choice view the pilot as an important opportunity to determine if an ACO organized by a network connected *not* by ownership or true information technology (IT) integration can have an impact on moderating costs and improving quality. Both project sponsors believe this is a more realistic pilot that has greater application to the "masses" than other pilots undertaken in other areas. Their attitude is "if you can do it here, you can do it anywhere."

Geisinger Health System

William Breen, Jr.

The Geisinger Health System (GHS) is a healthcare system operating in northeastern and central Pennsylvania with headquarters located in Danville, Pennsylvania. GHS was formed in 1915 by Abigail Geisinger, widow of iron magnate George Geisinger, who used her fortune to build a hospital intended to be a regional medical center modeled on the Mayo Clinic. The GHS today enjoys national recognition as a model for high-quality integrated health service delivery and is known as one of the Best Hospitals in America; its physicians have also been listed in The Best Doctors in America. The Geisinger Medical Center, located in Danville, with two other hospitals in Wilkes-Barre—Geisinger Wyoming Valley and Geisinger South Wilkes-Barre—is its primary care facility. There are a large number of Geisinger clinics located throughout northeastern Pennsylvania in Wilkes-Barre, Pittston, Wyoming, Scranton, Dallas, Plains, Kingston, and other surrounding cities and towns.

GSH has expressed that it operates around four very important themes: quality, value, partnerships, and advocacy. Its strategic priorities are quality and value, innovation, expanding the clinical market, and securing the legacy. GHS has always had great pride in its leadership during challenging complex and difficult times and was one of the first health systems to implement an electronic medical record (EMR). The GHS EMR effort, in place since 1996, provides patients the ability to view their records, electronically communicate with their caregivers, and research various medical topics through links to trusted medical information on the Internet. Non-GHS physicians and their staff can access their patients' GHS electronic health records (EHRs) by utilizing a special portal that allows them to communicate electronically with GHS specialists and subspecialists. GHS has adopted the Epic EMR for electronic documentation of patient and medical information. Currently, the latest implementation, known as Computerized Provider Order Entry (CPOE), took place at Geisinger Medical Center in mid-October 2007 and has remained a success.

Glenn J. Steele, Jr., MD, PhD, who arrived at GHS March 1, 2001, is the current chief executive officer of GHS. During his tenure, he has taken many initiatives to secure the hospital as well as expand the health system. In 2011, Dr. Steele unveiled his 2011–2015 Vision for Geisinger Health System, which includes the strategic priorities of quality and innovation and market leadership. GHS has enjoyed strong financial performance in recent years. In 2010, GHS ended the fiscal year with an operating income of $127.4 million (after interest expense). Revenue grew 10.7% from the prior year, and GHS provided $274.5 million of community benefits, including care provided under government programs at less than cost and other uncompensated care.

Leadership at GHS strongly believes that GHS is well positioned to benefit from the coming shifts in reimbursement methods. GHS views itself as a true integrated delivery system in which the physicians and hospital agree to take joint responsibility for keeping patients healthy and to share the financial benefits that result. Operating a large health plan in addition to large healthcare facilities, GHS is well positioned to benefit on the insurer side of the equation by lowering the cost of care. The system's integrated delivery system parallels the qualities of an ACO by integrating technology that enhances care and fosters innovation. It stresses collaboration and creates value.

The building blocks laid by leadership, including a strong culture of interdisciplinary collaboration and quality efforts, led GHS to develop a radical way of approaching value on behalf of its patients and those that pay for the cost of care. In February 2006, Geisinger launched a new program with the intent of changing how healthcare is provided and paid for in the United States. Called *ProvenCare* by GHS, the program features three key elements: a strict reliance on evidence-based standards in medicine, a fixed-price financial mechanism to pay for certain procedures (such as open heart surgery), and patient engagement/activation. GHS says the program is an attempt to give patients the most consistent, comprehensive, and effective care possible.

ProvenCare could not be successful without the adherence to acute episodic models of care that greatly reduce variation in treatments by adhering to evidenced-based standards. These operate in the acute care setting as well as physicians' offices, home, and other settings. GHS has chosen to tackle chronic disease as a major focus of reducing variation. The diseases chosen were those that caused the greatest morbidity and include diabetes, congestive heart failure, coronary artery disease, hypertension, and a prevention bundle. Geisinger has leveraged the EMR to drive this collaboration and to ensure there are no gaps in care that may lead to increased morbidity.

Based on the ability of ProvenCare to reduce variation and improve quality, Medicare (Centers for Medicare and Medicaid Services, CMS) launched a shared-savings program with GSH in January 2012. Simply stated, the project's goal is to bend the cost curve. Savings achieved beyond the joint target set by GSH and CMS will be shared with GSH's Integrated Delivery Network. This network has the ability to (1) accept accountability for achieving this target, (2) participate for a minimum of 3 years, (3) adopt a legal structure to distribute any savings to providers, and (4) include a sufficient number of PCPs to serve a minimum of 5000 beneficiaries.

By operating a large health plan, GSH has the ability to use its enterprise to bridge the provider, patient, and payer relationship with engagement and focus on improving patient access and health status. A collaborative between the Geisinger Health Plan (GHP) and the GSH physician clinics is the ProvenCare navigator system. Under this model, ProvenCare navigators work in physicians' offices to assist patient care according to evidenced-based protocols for chronic diseases that drive cost and quality. The GHP employs over 61 case managers at 31 community practice sites. Early results attained in the first 3 years of the program claimed impressive results, with a 40% reduction in 30-day readmissions and a 20% reduction in overall admissions to the facility. The protocols followed by the case managers are evidenced based, patient centered, and physician guided.

As with any case study for innovation, it may be true that the exact building blocks employed or created by GSH might be more difficult or nonexistent at other facilities. But, the principals by which GSH operates and the impressive results they are achieving are a beacon to those searching for solutions.

Piedmont Healthcare's Integration Strategy

James Sams, MD

Medical Director, Piedmont Healthcare

Piedmont Healthcare's (PHC's) history in Atlanta, Georgia, began over 100 years ago. Drs. Ludwig Amster and Floyd McRae opened Piedmont Hospital in 1905 on Capital Avenue. In 1956, the hospital was relocated to its current location at Peachtree Street and Collier Road. The organization now includes five hospitals and two employed physician entities. The organization also houses a PHO that includes all five hospitals and employed and independent physicians. PHC is moving from a hospital holding company to an integrated healthcare delivery system.

PHC is pursuing a multifaceted approach to position itself uniquely in the Atlanta market. The Piedmont Clinic (PHO) was established as an early effort to integrate the hospital and medical staff. The clinic has single-signature authority for all of the major commercial contracts for its members, both employed and independent. A model of financial integration was initially used to enable the contracting activities of the hospitals, primary care, and specialty physicians. This was a primitive way to allow joint contracting with the hospitals and physicians. A large penalty was accessed on the joint contracts based on quality metrics. The metrics were relatively crude and not truly population based. The scale of the penalties was destabilizing and counterproductive. It was difficult to move the discussions away from the money so the focus could be on the care.

In 2009, the clinic board elected to transition the group to a clinically integrated model to prepare the group for the future of population management and value-based purchasing. This strategy produced the need for a new quality platform to enable disparate groups to come together around the populations they serve. The data requirements necessary to support true population metrics were extensive. There still remains a portion of financial risk spread across the quality metrics. It is enough to hold the physicians' attention while not detracting from the work around quality and care transformation. The ultimate penalty under clinical integration is expulsion from the clinic if a provider is unable to, after some remediation, perform to the quality benchmarks.

The new platform has to account for the different EMRs utilized not only by the employed groups but also by the independent physicians. Some of the groups were still using paper records, producing further challenges. A claims-based data warehouse was selected, and after review of what was commercially available, the clinic board elected to build this capability in-house. The existing vendors did not have the depth needed to support the new quality programs. It was decided that it could be built more quickly and at a competitive price. Claims from both physician members and the hospitals are submitted electronically to the warehouse. The analytics are producing both patient-level and population-level dashboards on the quality metrics selected for action. The warehouse holds 18 months of data. The stage is set for the transition to value. The clinic operates in a pure fee-for-service environment currently and is discussing alternative contracting strategies for the near future.

The employed groups offer different opportunities for integration and contracting. The Piedmont Physician Group (PPG) has 150 doctors, most on a common EMR. The group operates on the standard clinic contracts. The group executed an addendum to the Cigna contract, creating what is referred to as a collaborative ACO. This is a medical home infrastructure with a shared-savings agreement providing an alternative payment methodology. A group of four care coordinators interact with data from Cigna, the clinic, and the EHR to engage patients and providers in activities that can potentially improve care and reduce cost. The shared-savings pool is determined by a combination of the total medical cost trend and quality performance. The other employed physicians at Piedmont are the cardiologists. They are on the same EHR as primary care. Efforts are under way to build care pathways for the common conditions treated by both groups. The goal is to engage the different specialty groups in the Clinic in building a medical neighborhood as described in the white paper of the American College of Physicians (ACP). As the model matures, the independent primary care physicians in the clinic can be engaged. The Piedmont Clinic will become the center for total care integration.

The healthcare system is also pursuing additional strategies for integrating care. In 2012, the first of the hospitals went live on Epic. Over the next 18 to 24 months, all five hospitals and all employed physician practices will be on this platform. Concurrently, a roll-out strategy to nonemployed clinic physicians is being planned. Eventually, it will be made available to all medical staff physicians. This IT strategy will produce further opportunities to align physicians and coordinate care. As the group develops expertise in managing populations, it will move into appropriate levels of risk contracting to leverage the value inherent in these activities.

While these strategies are easier to execute inside a pure employment structure, PHC feels that is important to maintain a mixed model to optimize its position in the Atlanta market. This strategy will enable it to build on the tradition of physician-led, patient-centric care as the system moves toward accountable, value-based care. To quote Dr. Don Berwick, "The angel is in the details."

Norton Healthcare System

Ginger Figg

President, Norton Physician Services

Norton Healthcare has a 125-year, faith-based history of providing care to the Louisville community. The health system is made up of five hospitals, including Kentucky's only full-sevice, free-standing pediatric hospital, 12 immediate care centers, more than 140 physician practice locations, and nearly 600 employed physicians.

Norton Healthcare is a regional leader in primary care, cardiology, women's services, orthopedics, neurosurgery, oncology, and pediatrics. It is also a pilot site, in partnership with Humana, for the Accountable Care Organization (ACO) model through the Brookings–Dartmouth ACO Pilot Project.

Norton Healthcare's physician employment model was established in 1995, with approximately 14 primary care physicians. The goal was to acquire and develop insurance panels associated with those physicians and work through capitation agreements. Prior to this time, the organization included downtown hospitals, oncology practices, several immediate care centers and affiliation agreements with regional hospitals. This plan did not transpire as expected because capitation did not become prevalent in the local market outside of Medicaid. At this point, Norton Healthcare acquired community hospitals from the Columbia system and created a large regional presence.

Norton's main campus includes Norton Hospital, recognized as a regional tertiary hospital, and Kosair Children's Hospital, a renowned pediatric hospital. The primary care physician (PCP) network played a key role in supporting the community hospitals, and Norton Healthcare added 40 primary care physicians over the next several years.

As more primary care physicians joined the system, private specialty physicians were attracted to it as well. As physician relationships developed, Norton Healthcare moved further into clinical integration to add employed specialty physicians and develop aggressive cardiovascular and cardiac surgery service lines, along with others.

With some changes in the marketplace, Norton Healthcare began acquiring pediatric, orthopedic, radiology, neurosurgery, and obstetric/gynecologic specialties to support the needs of downtown and suburban communities. This strategy proved successful in building strong service lines with a co-management philosophy. At this point, Norton Healthcare had approximately 60% specialties and 40% primary care under the Norton umbrella.

Norton Healthcare was careful to maintain its relationships with private physicians. As long as the physicians were supported, it was strongly encouraged that referrals from employed physicians went to private physicians as well as employed physicians. At this point, the payers were fee for service, and new payment mechanisms were only employed in small pilots.

In 2010, Norton Healthcare entered into an Accountable Care Organization (ACO) model through the Brookings–Dartmouth ACO Pilot Project to build an accountable care/integrated health care model, initially with Norton Healthcare employees and subsequently with Humana employees. By mid-2012, there were 7,500 insured individuals with a shared-savings financial model.

In this pilot, more diabetic patients were tested for blood sugar control and cholesterol management in the first year of participation. Blood sugar testing among diabetic patients increased from 87.7% in the baseline year to 93.4%, and cholesterol management tests climbed from 83.9% to 91.8%.

Norton Healthcare and Humana agreed to share savings beyond an initial 2% reduction in costs for patients included in the pilot. Norton Healthcare is not liable for losses should healthcare costs accelerate instead of slow.

Norton Healthcare planned for a move toward an integrated IT system with Epic electronic medical records (EMR) system in approximately 53 offices initially, and then in all of the physicians' offices by the end of 2012, followed by all Norton Healthcare hospitals by early 2013.

In 2012, employed physicians were paid by various methods. Generally, this is by a collection model with additional quality and outcomes metrics (as pay for performance) on top of that. On the specialty side, it is a collection model or a work relative value unit model. Again, some of these groups have quality initiatives and some are evolving.

Overall, the plan is to increase the integration among primary care physicians and specialists using the Epic EMR system as a backbone. Norton Healthcare also has significant plans to expand the Dartmouth–Brookings ACO pilot and increase incentive payment structures.

Summa Health System

Nancy A. Myers, PhD

System Director, Quality/Clinical Effectiveness

Summa Health System is an integrated healthcare delivery system that provides coordinated, value-based care across the continuum for the populations it serves. Headquartered in Akron, Ohio, Summa Health System employs nearly 11,000 staff and healthcare professionals and includes seven owned, affiliated, and joint venture hospitals; a regional network of ambulatory centers; a network of more than 1300 physicians (Summa Health Network); an employed multi-specialty physician group (Summa Physicians, Inc.); a provider-owned health plan (SummaCare); an accountable care organization (NewHealth Collaborative); and a system-level foundation.

The System operates more than 2100 licensed inpatient beds on its campuses. Outpatient care is extended through four community health centers and through partnerships with various community entities. Three System hospitals offer accredited residency programs partnering with statewide medical and podiatry schools; two of the campuses in the System, Summa Akron City and St. Thomas Hospitals, are teaching affiliates of the Northeastern Ohio Medical University, housing 17 accredited residency and fellowship training programs.

The System has a long history of success in building community partnerships to improve care coordination for its patients. For example, its Senior Services Institute partners with community-based services through the Area Agency on Aging 10B, Incorporated (AAoA) to ensure the medical and wellness needs of low-income seniors are met before and after hospitalization. The Summa Health System/AAoA partnership for Geriatric Care Excellence is an interdisciplinary collaboration between Senior Services and the AAoA that helps frail, low-income seniors living in the community to receive community-based long-term care services. The collaboration includes AAoA nurses on site at every Summa Health System hospital to screen and arrange for services to support patients postdischarge as well as collaborative development of an individualized plan of care by hospital discharge planning staff and AAoA case managers. For patients requiring skilled nursing facility care, the Senior Services Institute's Care Coordination Network is a collaborative with 40 community nursing facilities working to improve care transitions between hospitals and nursing facilities. The Senior Services Institute also provides transitional care models covering patients from hospital to home using registered nurses for targeted diagnoses, a transitional model from the skilled geriatric rehabilitation units using nurse practitioners, and a model from hospital to home involving hospital staff working with patients/families in a patient activation model with a discharge follow-up call.

Summa's strategic priorities include advancing its clinical enterprise, achieving effective integration, and expanding its patient population base. Key to each of these priorities is the effective alignment and integration between System hospitals and facilities and its physicians—both employed and affiliated. It is accomplishing this goal through physician employment (Summa Physicians, Inc.), clinical integration (Summa Health Network), and the development of a provider-led ACO (NewHealth Collaborative).

Summa Physicians, Inc. (SPI) was founded in 1995 to promote stronger affiliation of physicians and provide a base of services for the communities that the System serves. It currently employs nearly 300 physicians in over 30 primary care and specialty practice areas. Patients benefit by being part of a group practice that includes a common electronic medical record (EMR), standards for access and patient satisfaction, and the ongoing development of innovative care practices. Physicians who are employees have access to and are served by the System's information technology (IT) resources, quality and process improvement personnel, legal and regulatory expertise, and strong brand identity. SPI continues to recruit new physicians into its employed practice model and is focused on expanding processes and resources to facilitate enhanced coordination of patient-centered care among and between its providers, including the development of standardized referral processes and information flow between primary care and specialty care physicians and the development of patient-centered medical homes in its primary care offices.

The Summa Health Network (SHN), a physician hospital organization, works with over 1300 physician and advance practice nurse members and all of the System hospitals to provide contracting services with regional and national payers as part of its "messenger model." Beginning in 2005, SHN launched a program to assist physicians with the implementation of EMR systems in their offices with the goal of moving toward so-called "clinical integration." Physicians were provided with financial assistance (more than $2.1 million were awarded to SHN affiliated practices in exchange for agreeing to share data with the network) and IT implementation support. SHN maintains the master agreement with the EMR provider and provides locally hosted servers stored in a secure data center with management of maintenance and updates for its members. Physicians participating with SHN receive assistance in achieving meaningful use standards, and their record systems interface with the Summa Health System hospitals. Over 700 physician members receive this EMR implementation support.

Using this IT has made it possible for SHN to negotiate performance incentive payment models for its physicians with several payers in the market. It has also allowed SHN to work with its physicians to develop an ambulatory care model to identify areas for focused improvement, introduce evidence-based best practices into the clinical office settings using the EMR, and provide report cards to providers to track their improvements. Providers also receive periodic reports identifying patient-specific care opportunities for both preventive services and chronic illness management.

Building on the success of the Summa Health Network, Summa Health System entered into a new partnership with several community physician practices to found its accountable care organization: the NewHealth Collaborative (NHC). NHC began operations in 2011 and is a clinician-led collaborative that partners with communities to compassionately care for and serve their populations in an accountable-, value-, and evidence-based manner. NHC was established as a nonprofit, taxable organization with a board of directors comprised of member physicians (75%) and System leadership (25%). Its delivery network consists of approximately 450 primary and specialty care physicians and the System's hospitals and facilities; SummaCare, the System's health plan, partners with NHC to provide claims payment services, population data management support, and care management services.

Physician members of NHC agree to participate in the development and implementation of evidence-based care models and foundational care delivery redesign efforts. The NHC uses a shared-savings incentive model to reward providers for improved performance and to fund new infrastructure to support additional care delivery improvements. Its focus on care improvement is twofold: identification of focused care opportunities (including the development of condition-specific care models and enhanced support of patients at points of care transition) and the creation of foundational care systems that will improve outcomes and experience for patients across the continuum.

One of the key foundational delivery system changes that the NHC is driving within the System is the transformation of primary care practice sites into patient-centered medical homes (PCMHs).

The PCMH Initiative is a collaborative project between NHC and six community physician group practices to provide better value to patients by transforming their traditional practices into medical homes. The first wave of this initiative, which began in 2011, included 36% of NHC's primary care physicians; additional offices will be included in 2012–2013. A multidisciplinary PCMH task force led by NHC primary care physician board members was established and includes physicians, practice managers, office staff, administrative personnel, System process engineers, SummaCare staff, IT representatives, and operations analysts. Key team members received training on medical home models through participation at PCMH conferences (e.g., sponsored by American Academy of Family Physicians) and site visits to certified PCMH programs (e.g., Geisinger).

The participants of the initiative developed common principles for PCMH, including fundamental concepts of primary care (access, coordination, and communication), as well as new approaches for care delivery (including enhanced access; physician-directed, team-oriented practice; quality and safety monitoring). Using a quality science approach and Lean/Six Sigma tools, a process has been developed for medical home transformation according to these guiding principles and will be utilized by all NHC primary care physician practices to pursue medical home status.

Based on experience and outcomes obtained from the ongoing PCMH project, NHC will use a PCMH transformation framework that includes four project management phases: initiation, planning, execution, and monitoring for current and future medical homes.

The Summa Health System holds itself clinically and financially accountable for health outcomes in its communities. It has a history of partnership with community resources and an ongoing strategy for physician partnership and integration that includes employment and collaborative models of care. Its future development includes enhanced connectivity with its community of physicians through the development of a health information exchange and a clinical communications center to support its clinicians in their achievement of the triple aim of healthcare: enhanced patient experience, better patient outcomes, and lower costs.

Hospital Physician Integration: Baylor Health Care System

David J. Ballard, MD

Senior Vice President and Chief Quality Officer, Baylor Health Care System

Paul B. Convery, MD

Senior Vice President and Chief Medical Officer, Baylor Health Care System

The Baylor Health Care System (BHCS) has employed a broad range of hospital physician integration tactics since the organization began in 1903 as Baylor University Medical Center, which opened its doors with 25 beds. BHCS was legally formed in the early 1980s through the linkage of several hospitals in the Dallas Fort Worth Metroplex, and as a key tactic to advance hospital physician integration, the employed physician group of BHCS, the HealthTexas Provider Network (HTPN), was created in 1994. In 2012, BHCS had annual operating revenues exceeding

$4 billion, with 30 owned, leased, ventured, or affiliated hospitals; 26 jointly ventured surgical centers; 600 employed physicians; 20,000 other employees; and 4000 physicians on its hospital medical staffs.

One of BHCS's early explicit approaches to hospital physician integration was through the creation of a position of senior vice president for clinical integration in the early 1990s and the formation in 1994 of its first systemwide clinical committee, the BHCS Quality Council, chaired by John Anderson, MD, then senior vice president for clinical integration. An emphasis on quality continued to be one avenue to accelerate hospital physician integration for BHCS through the hiring in 1999 of its first chief quality officer, David Ballard, MD. By the end of 2000, BHCS's chief executive officer, Joel Allison, focused a new strategic planning effort around a vision to "become the most trusted source of comprehensive health services" by 2010 and, as one of its 10 strategic objectives, "to deliver the best and safest care available." As part of the BHCS strategic refocusing effort, Dale Jones, then the chair of the BHCS board of trustees, established in 2000 an Ad Hoc Quality Measurement Review Committee to identify key healthcare quality indicators and to make recommendations to measure and improve the quality of care. The committee, chaired by Dr. Ballard, laid out a healthcare improvement strategic plan for the organization based on three crucial elements: (1) the alignment of every board member across BHCS, as well as the BHCS frontline employees, toward making quality of care a priority; (2) the introduction of performance management incentives linked to clinical indicators; and (3) the creation of a multidisciplinary healthcare improvement operations team across all BHCS operating units.

Beginning in 2001, BHCS began to drive hospital physician integration and related quality improvement through its Best Care Physician Champion model. System-level and hospital-level physician champions provided the intellectual capital and leadership to teach and pioneer quality efforts throughout BHCS. These physicians motivated, encouraged, and offered medical expertise to collaboratively design solutions to address the challenges to quality improvement and to support standardization of evidence-based processes of care. Physician champions were identified in various specialties, including obstetrics, cardiology, patient safety, primary care, critical care, surgery, and geriatrics. Some of these physician champions transitioned to assume broader leadership roles as BHCS launched formal clinical service lines in 2008.

In 2006, to further enhance hospital physician integration, BHCS recruited its first chief medical officer (CMO), Paul Convery, MD. Among other leadership roles, Dr. Convery chairs the systemwide Physician Leadership Council and the CMO Operations Council and works with physician and operational leaders to advance hospital physician integration across the system. A few years after the creation of Dr. Convery's systemwide CMO role, BHCS developed vice president for medical affairs/CMO roles for each of its hospitals, such that by 2012 every hospital had in place a part-time or full-time vice president for medical affairs/CMO.

In conjunction with the founding of an employed medical group and the development of specific physician leadership positions to promote hospital physician integration, BHCS has invested heavily in the training of physician leaders. Building on the early work in rapid cycle quality improvement at BHCS that was led by HTPN primary care physicians and hospitalists, BHCS currently trains multi-disciplinary teams of hospital and other administrators and physicians and other clinicians in rapid cycle quality improvement. The curriculum introduces administrative and clinical leaders to quality improvement methods and ways to measure and analyze evaluations; helps them to understand the relationship between quality and cost; and provides a general understanding of statistical variation, the tools of patient safety, and leadership strategies for quality improvement. To date, more than 250 physicians and more than 1500 other BHCS personnel have completed the 60-hour face-to-face course. BHCS has also developed a physician leadership training program with Southern Methodist University's (SMU's) Cox School of Business, through which it trains cohorts of approximately 50 physicians every 2 years to become more effective in hospital leadership roles. A few of these physicians with particular promise in hospital and healthcare system leadership have been funded by BHCS to complete the full executive MBA program at SMU.

In addition to the creation and expansion of its employed physician group, its physician administrative leadership roles, and its training programs, BHCS has deployed a broad range of business relationships with physicians to advance hospital physician alignment. Several regional and national physician groups and physician management corporations were founded associated with BHCS, including Texas Oncology PA, the largest oncologic group practice in the United States, and EMCare, the largest emergency care and hospitalist physician services organization in the United States. BHCS has endeavored to advance hospital physician integration through many hospital physician joint venture relationships, including those through United Surgical Partners International and through two joint venture heart hospitals in which BHCS owns 51% and physician investors own 49%, the Baylor Heart and Vascular Hospital and the Heart Hospital Baylor Plano. Most recently, as a means to enable affiliated but independent physicians as well as BHCS employed physicians to be rewarded financially for both delivering high-quality care or improving care and reducing the cost of that care below what would otherwise be expected by Medicare or other payers, BHCS has created the Baylor Quality Alliance (BQA) as its accountable care organization (ACO). As the initial contract for the BHCS ACO, BQA plans to have BQA physicians and BHCS hospitals serve as the preferred providers for the care of the approximately 35,000 BHCS employees and their dependents beginning in 2013.

Bibliography

Annals of surgery, 246(4), October 2007. Lippincott, Williams & Wilkins.
Baylor Health Care System official website, www.baylorhealth.com
Gbemudu, Josette, and Bridget Larson, *Commonwealth Fund, Case Study Series*, January 2012.

Geisinger Health Systems official website, www.geisinger.org

Gerberry, Robert, *Digital ties that bind: EMRs and HH,* January 2012.

Healthcare Financial Management Association. *Case study: creating best care for patients,* HFMA, April 28, 2011. http://www.hfma.org/Publications/Leadership-Publication/Archives/Special-Reports/Spring-Summer-2011/Case-Study--Creating-Best-Care-for-Patients/

Little, Karen. *Patient centered primary care collaborative,* Cigna Healthcare, June 2010.

Methodist Le Bonheur Healthcare official website, www.methodisthealth.org

Norton Healthcare official website, www.nortonhealthcare.com

Piedmont Health Care official website, www.piedmont.org

Summa Health Systems official website, www.summahealth.org

Summa Foundation official website, www.summafoundation.org

Chapter 10

Putting It All Together: Full Integration

Introduction

As you may have gathered from the previous chapters, the solution to what is wrong with American healthcare is much more complex than simply encouraging physician and hospital integration. Although this is an important piece, much more must be done to improve healthcare delivery in this country. Integration of healthcare and healthcare delivery at all levels is critical to having efficient healthcare and great outcomes. We must focus on all areas of health, not simply healthcare delivery.

We all agree that the current costs and utilization trends are unsustainable. Fragmentation and misalignment of resources are leading to less quality of care than we should expect to achieve for the amount of money we are spending. There are multiple compelling financial priorities driving healthcare reform. The first is dealing with the ballooning federal budget deficit. A trillion dollar deficit is unsustainable and must be stabilized. Much of the federal budget is related to healthcare, particularly Medicare; therefore, the growth rate of healthcare spending associated with the graying of America must be moderated. With more people living longer and being burdened by more chronic diseases, we must move to new financial models.

In addition, we must take pressure off the state and federal budgets that support care of the uninsured and underinsured through Medicaid programs. Both of these programs are leading to an erosion of gross domestic product (GDP). Since this is a zero-sum game (other than the limited growth of GDP year after year), if a larger percentage is allocated to healthcare, the other budget needs (e.g., education, defense, and other global national issues) must share what is left.

Blurring of Boundaries

One of the trends we are seeing in healthcare is that there is a blurring of lines of demarcation between healthcare providers. Health insurers are buying hospitals, hospitals are buying physicians, and all stakeholders of healthcare are aligning with each other via ownership or alliance models.

> People who believe health care in this country is an actual system with systemic processes fully in place … the truth is there is almost total lack of systems thinking in health care. Health care is delivered one unit at a time. That is what the market incents.
>
> **—George Halvorson, Health Care Reform Now! 2007**

There is a breakdown of the customary and traditional roles between economic stakeholders, including insurers, hospitals, and physicians. New technologies are helping to enable this process and are providing a rapid consolidation of providers. To begin to address the cost of care, efficiency must be gained through these consolidation efforts and the blurring of traditional healthcare delivery roles. Hospital systems are also rapidly consolidating, and smaller hospitals are finding it difficult to maintain economies of scale. Many services in the hospital delivery system are subject to diminishing marginal returns; therefore, size is a critical competitive advantage. Many experts feel that to survive in the future healthcare environment, a healthcare system must be very large, and that smaller systems and individual hospitals will not exist.

This can also lead to additional economic leveraging of large health systems to the payers, demanding a higher reimbursement. This could slow the movement of healthcare efficiency if healthcare monopolies are formed and price competition cannot take place.

These three developments—the blurring of traditional healthcare delivery lines, industry consolidation, and health information exchanges—will change the healthcare delivery system as we know it.

Health versus Healthcare

Health as a concept is much bigger than healthcare delivery, which is the topic we have been discussing. As you can see from Figure 10.1, only 10% of health is actually attributed to healthcare delivery. There are many genetic, environmental, and socioeconomic factors that contribute to overall health. To achieve optimal health and control healthcare costs, we cannot ignore these factors. Environmental and socioeconomic factors contribute directly and indirectly to healthcare expenditures. We also must as a society make the crucial decision on whether healthcare is a social

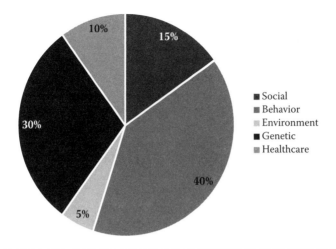

Figure 10.1 The leading determinants of health. (From McGinnis, J. M., et al. The case for more active policy attention to health promotion. *Health Affairs (Millwood),* **21(2): 79–93 (2002).**

right or a privilege. Currently, it is treated mostly as a privilege. However, there are many safety net hospitals and clinics that make an argument that it is an inalienable right. This is the societal question that will have to be solved as healthcare reforms progress. At this point, the individual mandate was upheld by the Supreme Court. This decision will help set a course of healthcare reform.

To achieve optimum and efficient healthcare, integration must take place, including both financial and clinical information. It also must include creating a culture that rewards and encourages health and a system that is seamless and aligned in healthcare delivery. In truth, everyone must engage in the solution.

Performance-Based System

We are moving from a utilization-based system, in which each visit is paid based on volume, to a performance-based system, in which physicians are paid on achieving positive outcomes (Figure 10.2). This is the only way that we can aggressively and sustainably attack the cost curve. This will require disruptive innovation and is extremely difficult in a world where we have to have one foot in one system and one foot in the other. Some of the current experiments have failed and many of the future experiments will continue to fail. Some of the changes are too subtle and do not truly reward change in a meaningful way. Much like the days when practices had some of their patients on a capitated model, trying to manage two different incentive processes is difficult.

	Old Model	*Future Model*
Financial incentives	Encounter numbers	Outcomes
Visit focus	Face-to-face	Team care
income	Volume based	Outcome based
Patient satisfaction	Secondary factor	Tied to reimbursement
Medical information	Isolated	Transparent
Consultants	Referral	Part of care system

Figure 10.2   Old model/new model.

The current payment model does not support changing healthcare delivery even with the adjunct of pay-for-performance and other outcomes-based payment models. We are just nipping the surface of the change that has to occur.

Demographic and Environmental Factors

Demographics will be changing this model dramatically with the "graying" of America (Figure 10.3). According to Deloitte and Touche in 2012, more Medicare beneficiaries will be using the system than people paying into the system (Social Security). This is a dramatic change from the recent past, when four people would pay into the system to cover the cost of one Social Security recipient. An additional

Implications
• More medical care in the home
• Increase telemonitoring
• Increased emphasis on palliative care and end-of-life care
• Increase in health aides and home support services
• More nursing homes, community care, and geriatric centers
• More nurse practitioners and physician assistants

Figure 10.3   Demographics will be changing this model dramatically with the "graying" of America. According to Deloitte and Touche in 2012, more Medicare beneficiaries will be using the system than people paying into the system (Social Security).

demographic change is that over half of all disposable income will be in the hands of seniors. There is also an issue of compression of morbidity because we are better able to manage chronic diseases; people are living longer with multiple chronic conditions, which are compressed within a smaller period of time. We also have a significant lack of geriatric specialists and a lack of a geriatric orientation in our healthcare system. We will have to deal with the end-of-life issues and the challenge of palliative care. So many healthcare dollars are spent in the last few months of life, when in many cases the quality of life is not carefully evaluated. How we deal with this will philosophically guide healthcare. Unfortunately, these issues are prone to political demagoguery and opportunism, making it more difficult to make societal decisions.

Besides the dramatic shortage of geriatricians, we are seeing a significant shortage of primary care physicians. The new care model will push individuals to practice at the top of their license, and we will have to come to an understanding of what role nurse practitioners and physician assistants can play in a team-based healthcare system. We must provide primary care for all who need it. This new "team-based" approach to healthcare will change the way we educate physicians and other healthcare providers. The current system rewards independence and individual decision making. This will have to change for progress to be achieved.

Legal Environment

We will have to modify the legal system to support these new models of care as well as modify the medical malpractice system, both of which contribute to increasing inefficiency and costs in our healthcare system. Many of these new models require data sharing and internal referrals. They promote gain sharing and help to meld for-profit with not-for-profit companies. Many laws prohibit this or make the structure to make these work unnecessarily complicated. They add cost and complexity to a system that is already overburdened.

Whether you are a believer in defensive medicine or not, one cannot deny that there is significant time, income, and anxiety that go into our current litigation-based malpractice system. We often reward plaintiffs who have bad outcomes, we have 1-800-bad drug hotlines, and we have nursing homes that cannot afford malpractice insurance. It is all but certain that all of these factors contribute to the cost of healthcare.

Metrics and Transparency

A successful new system will also require metrics and transparency. Our current reimbursement and billing structure is incredibly difficult to understand even for those of us who have been doing it for years. The idea of "reasonable-and-customary fees," fee schedules, formularies, and the like, all different for different health plans, is confusing and clouds many of the inadequacies of our system. Fees are set to maximize reimbursement and confuse noncontracted payers. Private-pay patients are forced to pay retail.

The current payment system is also designed to cost shift. Some providers lose money treating Medicare patients, and most lose money treating Medicaid patients. Almost all providers lose money with self-pay individuals since few patients can afford to pay for their own healthcare costs. Because of these challenges, hospitals and other providers must charge commercial payers a premium to cover the costs of these less-profitable payers. This is an indirect tax on the employers that are paying commercial premiums. This situation is making it harder and harder for these employers to compete in an international marketplace. Many other countries have better controls on healthcare expenditures. As costs increase, there are more individuals uninsured or underinsured. As hospitals and health systems see more of these patients, they must increase their fees to commercial patients to compensate for these patients. As this trend increases, eventually the premiums for commercial payers will become unsustainable. This can become a death spiral.

We must achieve transparency on what things cost and what value is derived. However, calculating cost is not easy. Calculating value is even harder. Value takes into account outcomes and access as well as satisfaction. One of the challenges is that comparing these variables in healthcare is difficult since few have complete information. This requires an infrastructure that can track and trend metrics of process and outcomes, as well as track patients through the system.

Population Health

Population health has been defined as the "health outcomes of a group of individuals including the distribution of such outcomes within the group." As we move from our sickness-based system dealing with acute care and to prevention, wellness, and avoidable acute care visits, we must move into the area of population health. From a population perspective, health has not been defined as a state free of disease (which is a current health delivery system definition), but as the capacity of people to feel, adapt, and respond to and control life's challenges and changes. This gets into the area of productivity and "feeling good," not just health and healthcare delivery.

In this approach, we aim to achieve the health of an entire population that includes prevention and wellness. One major challenge is to continue dealing with healthcare inequities among various population groups, such as environmental social structure, distribution, and so on, which are all important parts of this equation.

Socioeconomic status has been linked to population health. There is a social economic gradient with individuals with lower social economic status struggling for health even when the delivery system is the same. As we move into the area of population and health management, we are looking at dealing with patients

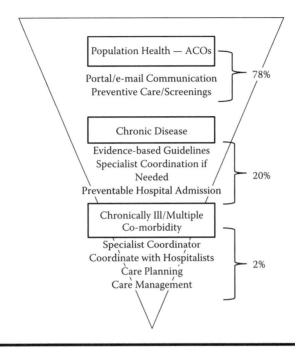

Figure 10.4 Typical family care physician 2500-patient panel.

who are not necessarily in the healthcare system now but will need to have their prevention and wellness managed even though they may not be seen at the classic physician's office (Figure 10.4). The focus here is to maintain or improve health and prevent costly, avoidable illness and unnecessary healthcare visits. This is the focus of accountable care arrangements and takes us a bit back to the health maintenance organizations (HMOs) of the 1980s and 1990s, for which prevention and avoiding expensive healthcare were the aims.

Physician Leadership

Healthcare in the future will require physician leadership. Physicians are typically not trained in business or leadership. Clinicians will have to make decisions on cost-effective care, taking to account the potential for improvement as well as the cost of therapy. Care models will have to be developed as well as care protocols. This will require physician leadership sitting at the same table with business leaders.

Since physicians are typically not trained in business or leadership, this will require different skill sets. Physician leadership was different in the past, when physicians were typically male, the doctor–patient model was parochial in nature, and life balance considerations were not critical. In a new model, physicians tend to look at things very differently. There are many more female physicians, particularly in primary care and family practice. Life–family balances are becoming increasingly critical to all physicians. Even the physician–patient relationship is changing, with more emphasis on a shared decision model than the classic patriarchal model. Physicians must be trained in these new leadership skills and sit across the table with policy makers and hospital and practice administrators and have a conversation using the same language. This will be a steep learning curve. They must also learn to work in a team-based environment.

Patient Engagement

Patients must be accountable for their own personal health. Recognizing that much of health is genetic or environmental, there are significant environmental factors that can be impacted by the patient. With many in the population expected to be diabetic in the near future secondary to obesity, individuals must be made responsible for the things they can control. Healthcare prevention must be encouraged and rewarded.

Patient engagement must take the form of financial responsibility. In the current delivery system, patients are insulated from the cost of healthcare by third-party payers. They typically pay only a copay or coinsurance. They often have no idea what things really cost. In some of the new high-deductible plans, patients must face the reality of their own healthcare costs. They still do not obtain accurate pricing, and there are not many discount programs for cash. They are forced to make decisions on preventive care and other healthcare decisions regarding services that they will pay for out of pocket without detailed facts.

They should benefit from transparency so they can pick the best and most efficient provider. Getting to transparency will be a complicated process (Figure 10.5).

• 55% looked online for treatment options (57% in 2009).
• 25% looked online for physician quality-of-care info.
• 12% used Internet for cost of providers.
• Gen X and Baby Boomers are most likely to use healthcare sites:
• 13% switched physicians last year (cost and quality).
• 34% would use a retail/walk-in clinic—16% already have.
• 29% said they would use a retail clinic immediately if they had to wait 1 week for a doc appointment.

Figure 10.5 Healthcare survey roundup. (From Deloitte's 2010 Survey of Health Care Consumers. With permission.)

Currently, we have a "sick" system that rewards healthcare providers for treating patients who are ill or have diseases. The system does not reward prevention or wellness. We must encourage and pay for outcomes and results in performance and not simply for activity.

Transformation

Care model transformation is a difficult process, and current financing models and payment schemes do not support it. Currently, non-face-to-face time with a physician is not compensated. In addition, novel interface systems with patients are not reimbursed, such as telephonic consultation with the patient or a consultant, home monitoring, or home management. Other things, such as group visits and e-visits, are also not consistently reimbursed. Many of these non-face-to-face interactions with the physicians are value added and have been shown to prevent more expensive costs down the road. Our current system only pays for volume-based care as opposed to outcomes or quality. As long as the reimbursement system does not support paying for these services, it is difficult for hospitals, physician practices, or integrated delivery systems to make the changes necessary and support themselves financially.

What seems clear is that these operational changes and financial reimbursement models must occur in sequence, with one change leading to the other, leading to the next. In other words, the financial changes will have to happen in sequence and in tandem to promote the care management changes. Only in this lockstep manner can physicians and delivery systems make the necessary changes. The only other option would be a disruptive innovation that would set up a major financial change, such as global payments, which could then support the delivery system changes necessary.

In the current model, should a delivery system want to move out in front of the care transformation process, it will be providing care that will not be reimbursed. Unless a provider owns the insurance entity and benefits from this lower cost, this is not a financial model for success. This is one of the frustrating things in healthcare: early innovators often do not survive the financial constructs of their new models.

One can certainly envision a scenario down the road in which payer pressures to reduce healthcare costs drive increasing efficiencies. This payer pressure ultimately comes from taxpayers through Medicare, Medicaid, and other federal funding sources; it will also come through employers. Large employers or small employers must drive decreasing healthcare costs to moderate and decrease their premium contributions. With this increasing pressure, new payment models must be developed, which will then push more improvement in healthcare delivery (Figure 10.6).

This will need to be assisted by electronic health records and information transparency so that these new shared reimbursement mechanisms (such as capitation

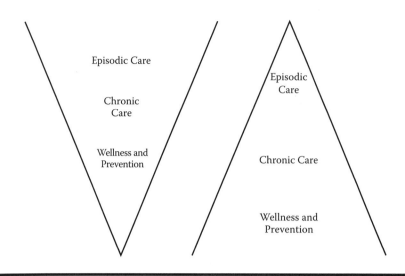

Episodic Care

Chronic Care

Wellness and Prevention

Episodic Care

Chronic Care

Wellness and Prevention

Figure 10.6   Healthcare triangle: moving toward population health.

or global payment models) will unite hospitals, physicians, and other healthcare providers into a single delivery system. In such an environment, each person will be knowledge rich with understanding of the different parts of the patient care model.

In this scenario, insurance companies may prove to be information managers, sharing detailed medical information across the care continuum, while providers have decision support and evidence-based care models that lead to better patient outcomes in these integrated delivery systems. Evidenced-based care with information technology (IT) systems that support this decision making will become the standard.

Size and scale will be critical. Hospitals, physicians, and others will form closer unions and collaborative models to provide the best care possible (Figure 10.7).

People love progress—it is change they don't like.

—Will Rogers

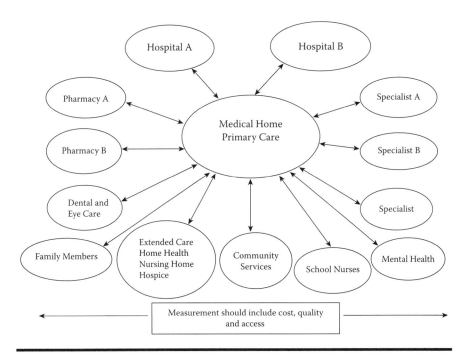

Figure 10.7 Care coordination ring. Patient-centered medical neighborhood. Measurement should include cost, quality, and access.

Bibliography

ACA imperative for accountability. 2010. Chart. http://www.sg2.com

Advisory Board Company. Transitioning from independent to interdependent. 203988. 2010. Chart. http://www.thehealthcareadvisoryboard.com.

Ahlquist, Gary, Gil Irwin, Minoo Javamardian, and Jack Topdjian. booz&co.

Aligned physicians find innovative ways to change behavior. 2010. Chart. http://www.sg2.com.

American Hospital Association. Clinical integration—the key to real reform. *Trend Watch*, February 2010. http://www.aha.org/research/reports/tw/10feb-clinicinteg.pdf

Arizona Hospital and Healthcare Association, St. Luke's Health Initiatives. Can this marriage be saved? Physician-hospital relationships. *Arizona Health Futures*, December 2005. http://slhi.org/pdfs/policy_primers/pp-2005-12.pdf.

BlueCross BlueShield of Texas. PCMH: pay for value-added activities. Experience Wellness Everywhere. http://www.bcbstx.com

BlueCross BlueShield of Texas. Where is the greatest potential for new value creation with providers? Chart, Experience Wellness Everywhere. http://www.bcbstx.com

Caramenico, Alicia. Hospital at home and integrated care improves quality, savings, November 1, 2011, www.fiercehealthcare.com, http://www.fiercehealthcare.com/story/hospital-home-integrated-care-improves-quality-savings/2011-11-01

Centers for Disease Control and Prevention, National Center of Health Statistics, National Vital Statistics System. Life expectancy at ages 65 and 85, by sex, selected years 1900–2001. Chart. http://www.cdc.gov

Connolly, Ceci, Jesse Bradford, and Beth Parish. Administration releases proposed rules for Medicare Accountable Care Organizations, McKinsey Center for US Health System Reform, April 1, 2011, http://healthreform.mckinsey.com/insights/reform_center_health_intelligence/administration_releases_proposed_rules

Deloitte and Touche. Healthcare survey roundup. 2010 Survey of Health Care Consumers. http://www.deloitte.com/assets/Dcom-UnitedStates/Local%20Assets/Documents/US_CHS_2010SurveyofHealthCareConsumers_050610.pdf

Eight Key Issues for Population Health Management in 2012, www.healthcareitnews.com/ http://www.healthcareitnews.com/news/8-key-issues-population-health-management-2012

Enhancing hospital-physician alignment. CEO Survey, *Healthcare Executive*, November/December 2011. Chart. http://www.ache.org.

Essential elements for 21st century health care. Chart.

Frommer, Leonard. Top ten DRGs 2010. Chart. September 2011.

Greater integration is also associated with higher revenue and profits. July 2009. Chart. http://www.sg2.com

Health Administration Press, A division of the Foundation of the American College of Healthcare Executives, *FutureScan 2012* www.ache.org, http://www.google.com/search?sourceid=navclient&ie=UTF-8&rlz=1T4ADFA_enUS443US444&q=FutureScan+2012

Health Care Advisory Board. Establishing the medical perimeter. Interviews and analysis, 21698A. 2011. http://www.thehealthcareadvisoryboard.com

Health Care Advisory Board. Limited to two viable models. 203988. 2010. http://www.thehealthcareadvisoryboard.com

Health Care Advisory Board. In need of a hospital-physician performance platform. 203988. 2010. http://www.thehealthcareadvisoryboard.com

Health Care Advisory Board. Range of options to align with independents. Interviews and analysis. www.thehealthcareadvisoryboard.com http://www.advisory.com/~/media/Advisory-com/Research/HCAB/Research-Study/2010/Accountable-Physician-Enterprise/The-Accountable-Physician-Enterprise-HCAB.pdf

Identify best-fit alignment options and timing. Chart 2010. http://www.sg2.com.

Kindig, D. What is population health? *American Journal of Public Health*, 93(3), 2003. www.ncbi.nlm.nih.gov

Kliff, Sara. Success of health reform hinges on hiring 30,000 primary care doctors by 2015, *Washington Post*, February 20, 2012, http://www.washingtonpost.com/business/success-of-health-reform-hinges-on-hiring-30000-primary-care-doctors-by-2015/2012/02/06/gIQAnslQ4Q_story.html

Managing Population Health, www.hhnmag.com/ October, 10, 2010, http://www.hhnmag.com/hhnmag/jsp/articledisplay.jsp?dcrpath=HHNMAG/Article/data/10OCT2010/1010HHN_Coverstory&domain=HHNMAG

McGinnis, J. M., et al. The case for more active policy attention to health promotion. *Health Affairs (Millwood),* 21(2): 79–93 (2002). Archived and available at http://www.healthaffairs.org.

Minich-Pourshadi, Karen, for HealthLeaders Media, The Business and Clinical Path to Medical Home, February 27, 2012. www.healthleadersmedia.com/ http://www.hcmarketplace.com/prod-9848/The-Business-and-Clinical-Path-to-Medical-Home.html

National Quality Forum. Performance measurement: NQF episode measurement framework. Chart. http://www.qualityforuum.org/projects/episodes_of_care_framework.aspx

Nursing shortages. Deloitte 2010 Survey of Health Care. http://www.healthaffairs.org

One definition of a medical home. Chart, from authors of Joint Principles of the PCMH and Guidelines for PCMH Recognition and Accreditation Programs, released by the AAFP, AAP, ACP, and AOA in 2007 and 2011. http://www.aafp.org

Oregon Health Authority. Challenge. Chart. http://www.oregon.gov/OHA/.

Population health, Wikipedia, the free encyclopedia, March 2012, http://en.wikipedia.org/wiki/Population_health

Sachs, Michael and Steven Lefar, *The Sg2 Letter*, 9(1), 2012, www.sg2.com/ http://members.sg2.com/content-detail-standard/?ContentID=80968445142856888663

Serio, Catherine D., and Ted Epperly. Physician leadership: a new model for a new generation. *Family Practice Management*, 13(2): 51–54 (2006). http://www.aafp.org/fpm/2006/0200/p51.html

Shifting environment demands a new approach to value creation and management. 2010. Chart. http://www.sg2.com

Society for Healthcare Strategy and Marketing Development. *FutureScan 2012*. Chicago: Health Administration Press, 2011. http://www.ache.org.

Tuso, Philip J. Physicians as leaders: the physician as leader. *Permanent Journal*, 7(1) (Winter 2003). http://xnet.kp.org/permanentejournal/winter03/leader.html.

Valentine, Steven T. 10 Trends for 2012, January 11, 2012, http://www.governanceinstitute.com/ResearchPublications/ResourceLibrary/tabid/185/CategoryID/1/List/1/catpage-index/3/Level/a/ProductID/1219/Default.aspx?txtSearch=growth+in+the+reform+er&SortField=DateCreated+DESC%2CDateCreated+DESC&ProductName=+&Free1=+

Index

A

accountable care organizations (ACOs)
   accounting system, 83
   accreditation process, 82
   care management, 83
   characteristics, 81–83
   clinical integration, 68
   data, 84
   financial incentives, 85
   governance, 58
   historical developments, 79
   "HMOs in drag," 79
   infrastructure, 85
   meaningful use, 76–77
   Medicare definition, 82
   models, 80–81
   Norton Healthcare System, 110–112
   overview, x, 79–80
   patient-centered focus, 83
   patient-centered medical home, 92
   patient engagement, 84
   payment experiments, 82, 83
   physician hospital organization, 35, 38
   Piedmont Healthcare, 109–110
   population health management, 84
   risk, 85
   savings opportunities, 86
   shift in treatment, 85
   startup cost, 81
   Summa Health Systems, 112–115
   technology developments, 84
accounting systems, 83
accreditation
   accountable care organizations, 82
   patient-centered medical home, 88
ACP, see American College of Physicians (ACP)
activities allowed, 36–37

advantages and benefits
   clinical co-management, 30–31, 33
   selling a medical practice, 49
advertising pharmaceuticals, 6
age distribution, 8, 9
agreements, see also Contracts
   employment considerations, 47
   hospital side, 50–51
   integration, 56
   medical directorships, 24
   physician side, 48–50
   physician view, 51
alignment models, 41–42
alignment strategy assessment
   balance sheet strength, 99
   bundled payments, 98
   competition alignment plans, 100
   competitive strength of facility, 100–101
   complexity of tactics, 102
   economic factors/drivers, 98
   employer position, 101–102
   external considerations, 98, 100
   fatigue, 99
   financial information, 99
   historical alignment position, 99
   hospital management talent, 98–99
   internal considerations, 98, 100
   key service lines, 97, 102
   knowledge, 97
   loyalty impact, 98
   management talent and resources, 98–99
   overview, 97
   payer needs and expectations, 101–102
   physician alignment strategy, 97–98
   physician readiness, 100
   primary care shortage, 101
   staff, 98–99
allowed activities, 36–37

American College of Physicians (ACP), 110
American College of Surgeons, 21
Amster, Ludwig, 109
ancillary services
    hospital billing, 45–46
    hospital viewpoint, 50
antikickback statutes and laws
    legal limitations, integration, 74
    medical directorships, 24
appraisal, private practice, 51, *see also* Valuation,
        private practice
assessment, *see* Alignment strategy assessment

B

balance sheet strength, 99
Ballard, David J., 115–117
Baylor Health Care System, 115–117
benchmarks, 44
benefits, 51, *see also* Advantages
Berwick, Don, 110
Billings Clinic, 74
Blue Cross and Blue Shield, 5
Blue Cross insurance, 5
board engagement, 63
books, writing, 49
boundaries, blurring of, 120
Breen, William R. (Bill), Jr., *xvi,* 105–108
Buffet, Warren, 11
bundled payments, *see also* Compensation;
        Payments and payment models
    alignment strategy, 98
    clinical co-management, 31
    clinical integration, 71–73
    future developments, 15
bylaws, current, 62

C

California Hospital Association, 26
call coverage, 25–27
capitation
    accountable care organizations, 85
    bundled payments, 73
    external, 41
    payment models, 60–61
    physician hospital organization, 38
cardiology alignment, 17
care coordination ring, 128–129
care management, 83
care redesign, 69–70

care transition, 8
Centers for Medicare and Medicaid Services
        (CMS), *see also* Medicaid; Medicare
    costs, accountable care organizations, 81
    fragmentation, 8
    medical directorships, 23, 24
    payment reforms, 71
challenges, co-management, 30–31
change *vs.* progress, 128
charitable care system, 5
charters, 57
Children's Health Insurance Program (CHIP), 9
CHIP, *see* Children's Health Insurance Program
        (CHIP)
Cigna Healthcare, 106
"claims-made" policy, 50
clinical co-management
    alignment model, 42
    benefits and challenges, 30–31
    effectiveness for service lines, 29–30
    example, 33–34
    overview, 29–33
    services, 33
    structure, 32
clinical institutes, 57
clinical integration
    bundled payments, 71–73
    care redesign, 69–70
    current state, 70
    defined, 69–71
    information technology, 75–77
    legal limitations, 73–75
    meaningful use, ACO, 76–77
    model, 68–69
    overview, *x,* 67–69
    payment models, 74–75
clinically integrated model, 36–37
clinical trials, 49
co-management, *see* Clinical co-management
communication, governance, 58
compensation, *see also* Bundled payments;
        Payments and payment models
    clinical co-management, 32
    hospital employment considerations, 50
competition alignment plans, 100
competitive strength of facility, 100–101
complexity
    of tactics, 102
    vs. integration models, 16
connectedness, 62
contracts, *see also* Agreements
    alignment model, 42

hospital employment, 50
integration model, 14
physician hospital organization, 36
Convery, Paul B., 115–117
costs
current issue of existing system, 10
historical developments, 6
shifting, 8, 10
culture
assessment tool, 62–63
employment considerations, 47
fit, 44–45
physician hospital organization, 35
current state
bylaws, cultural assessment tool, 62
clinical integration, 70

D

Darling v. Charleston Memorial Hospital, 21
data, 84
decade medical developments, 3–4
decision-making
physician employment, 48
physician employment agreements, 50
demographic factors
current healthcare system, 8–9
full integration, 122–123
demonstration project, 88
Department of Justice (DOJ)
independent practice associations, 34
legal limitations, integration, 72
departments, co-management, 30
DFRR, *see* Disclosure of Financial Relationship
Reports (DFRRs)
diagnosis related group (DRG)
bundled payments, 72
historical developments, 6
legal limitations, integration, 74
direct contract, 32
directorships, *see also* Medical directorships
alignment model, 42
integration model, 14
disadvantages
clinical co-management, 30–31
selling a medical practice, 49–50
Disclosure of Financial Relationship Reports
(DFRRs), 24
DOJ, *see* Department of Justice (DOJ)
"do more with less," 10
DRG, *see* Diagnosis related group (DRG)

drivers
clinical integration, 68
multiple factors and areas, 11
today's healthcare, 98

E

economics
employment, 45
factors/drivers, alignment strategy, 98
fit, physician hospital organization, 35
imperatives, 7–11
effectiveness, service lines, 29–30
e-health, 84
EHRs, *see* Electronic health records (EHRs)
electronic health records (EHRs)
clinical integration, 68
Piedmont Healthcare, 110
electronic medical records (EMR)
current healthcare system, 7–8
independent practice associations, 35
information technology, 75–76
Norton Healthcare System, 112
patient-centered medical home, 88
Piedmont Healthcare, 109
Summa Health Systems, 113
Emergency Medical Treatment and Active
Labor Act (EMTALA)
current healthcare system, 8
on-call expenditures, 25
employer position, 101–102
employment
agreements, 48–56
alignment models, 41–42
clinical institutes, 57
considerations, 46–48
cultural assessment tool, 62–63
cultural fit, 44–45
decision-making, 48
engagement difficulty assessment, 62–63
failure, 52
foundation model, 56
governance, 57–59
hospital side, 50–51
integration, 14, 56
making the decision, 48
metrics comparison, 50–52
overview, *x,* 41–46
payment models, 59–61
percentage Medicare reimbursement, 43
physician service agreements, 56–57
physician side, 48–50

physician view, 51
professional service agreements, 56–57
pros and cons, 49–51
"safe harbor," 43
specialties, 46
specialties, employment by, 45–46
EMR, *see* Electronic medical records (EMR)
EMTALA, *see* Emergency Medical Treatment
        and Active Labor Act (EMTALA)
engagement
        framework, 23
        full integration, 126–127
        physician employment, 62–63
entitlement programs, 10
environmental factors, 122–123
episode-based payments, 71–72, *see also*
        Bundled payments
example, co-management, 33–34
expenditures, national projection, 8, 9
expenditures per capita
        age comparisons, 9–10
        country comparisons, 1–2
        healthcare projections, 10–11
external considerations. alignment strategy, 98,
        100

F

facilities
        competitive strength of, 100–101
        hospital employment considerations, 51
failure, physician employment, 52
"fair market value" (FMV)
        clinical co-management, 31
        medical directorships, 24
        on-call coverage, 27
        valuation of practice, 44
fatigue, 99
Federal Trade Commission (FTC)
        legal limitations, integration, 72
        physician hospital organization, 37
Figg, Ginger, 110–112
financial alignment, 47
financial incentives, 85
financial information, 99
financially integrated model, 36–37
financial studies, 88, 90
firing staff, 51
Fisher, Elliott, 1, 79
fixed payment models, 59
foundation model, 56

fragmentation
        current healthcare system, 8
        healthcare delivery, 2
framework for engagement, 23
FTC, *see* Federal Trade Commission (FTC)
full integration
        blurring of boundaries, 120
        care coordination ring, 128–129
        demographic factors, 122–123
        environmental factors, 122–123
        "graying of America," 122–123
        healthcare survey, 126
        healthcare triangle, 127–128
        health *vs.* healthcare, 120–121
        leading determinants of health, 120–121
        legal environment, 122
        metrics, 123–124
        old model/new model, 121–122
        overview, 119
        patient engagement, 126–127
        performance-based system, 121–122
        physician leadership, 125–126
        population health, 124–125
        transformation, 127–128
        transparency, 123–124
        bundled payments, 15
        integration *vs.* complexity chart, 16
        overview, 13–16
        physician/hospital trust, 17–18
        types, 13–14
        vs. training, ix–x

G

Garfield, Sidney, 79
Geisinger Health System (GHS), 106–108
GHS, *see* Geisinger Health System (GHS)
governance, 57–59
"graying of America," 122–123
Great Depression, 5

H

Halvorson, George, 120
healthcare costs, shared savings model, 90, 91
healthcare delivery
        fragmentation, 2
        historical developments, 2–7
healthcare legislation issues, 10
healthcare survey, 126

healthcare system
  current structure, 7
  economic imperatives, 7–11
  fragmentation, 8
  historical perspectives, 2–7
  hospital-centric structure, 8
  issues, 8
  meaningful integration, *xii*
  overview, 1–2
healthcare triangle, 127–128
Health Choice, 106
Health Employer Data Information Set (HEDIS),
  60
health information exchanges (HIEs)
  clinical integration, 68
  information technology, 75–76
Health Information Portability Act (1996), 6
Health Information Technology for Economic
  and Clinical Health (HITECH), 69
health insurance exchange (HIE), 88
health maintenance organization (HMO)
  networks
  historical developments, 79
  "in drag," 79
  physician hospital organization, 36
health *vs.* healthcare, 120–121
HEDIS, *see* Health Employer Data Information
  Set (HEDIS)
HIE, *see* Health information exchanges (HIEs);
  Health insurance exchange (HIE)
hiring staff, 51
historical perspectives and developments
  alignment position, 99
  cultural engagement, 63
  decade developments, 3–6
  healthcare system, 2–7
  training, *ix–x*
HITECH, *see* Health Information Technology
  for Economic and Clinical Health
  (HITECH)
HMO, *see* Health maintenance organization
  (HMO) networks
"HMO's in drag," 79
home as hub, 88, 91
hospital billing, 45–46
hospital-centric structure, 8
hospital management talent, 98–99
hospital–medical group metrics, 52
hospital–physician integration, 115–117
hospital side, agreements, 50–51

hospital systems
  buying physician practices, 16, 17, 51
  and physician trust, 17–18
  selling to, 49–51
  workshop model, 6

I

IHI, *see* Initiative of Healthcare Improvement
  (IHI) Triple Aim
incentives
  historical developments, 7
  payment basis, 15, 17
  payment models, 59
  as problem, 11
independent practice associations (IPAs)
  governance, 57
  integration strategies, 13
Independent Practitioners Association (IPA),
  34–35
information technology (IT)
  clinical integration, 75–77
  patient-centered medical home, 88
  Summa Health Systems, 113–114
infrastructure, accountable care organizations, 85
Initiative of Healthcare Improvement (IHI)
  Triple Aim, 68
institutes, clinical, 57
insurance
  Blue Cross prepaid, 5
  prepaid plans, 5
  trends, 10
integration, *see also* Full integration
  agreements, 56
  goals, 67
  levels, 13–14
  methods and types, 13–14
  overview, *xi*
integration models, future developments
  bundled payments, 15
  types, 13–14
  vs. complexity chart, 16
integration models, traditional
  call coverage, 25–27
  medical directorships, 23–25
  medical staff, 21–22
internal considerations, 98, 100
Internal Revenue Service (IRS)
  Code Section 501(c)(3), 24
  legal limitations, integration, 74

medical directorships, 24
physician hospital organizations, 37
IPA, *see* Independent practice associations
(IPAs); Independent Practitioners
Association (IPA)
IT, *see* Information technology (IT)

J

job description, 49
Johnson v. Misericordia Hospital, 21
Joint Commission on Accreditation of
Healthcare Organizations (JCAHO),
21, 88
joint ventures
alignment model, 42
integration model, 14

K

Kaiser Permanente model, 79
key service lines, 97, 102
knowledge, alignment strategy, 97

L

leadership
Baylor Health Care System, 115–117
governance, 58
physician, 125–126
leading determinants of health, 120–121
leasing
alignment model, 42
integration model, 14
physician service agreements, 56–57
legal issues
full integration, 121
limitations, clinical integration, 73–75
structure, co-management, 30–31
legislation issues, 10
life expectancy impact, 6, 9
limited liability companies (LLCs), 33–34
locum tenens issues
on-call arrangements, 27
physician employment agreements, 49
longevity impact, 6, 9
loyalty
alignment strategy, 98
cultural assessment tool, 62
lumped payments, *see* Bundled payments

M

malpractice coverage, 50
management contracts, 42
management talent and resources, 98–99
mandatory entitlement programs, 10, *see also*
specific programs
Mayzell, George, *xv*
McRae, Floyd, 108
meaningful integration, *xii*
meaningful use, ACO, 76–77
measuring practice performance, 44
Medicaid, *see also* Centers for Medicare and
Medicaid Services (CMS)
historical developments, 6
as mandatory entitlement program, 10
medical directorships, *see also* Directorships
roles and responsibilities, 24–25
traditional integration models, 23–25
Medical Executive Committee (MEC)
authority, 63
medical group–hospital metrics, 52
Medical Group Management Association, 44
Medical Group Management Association
(MGMA)
governance, 58
on-call arrangements, 27
medical neighborhood, 93, 94
medical service organizations (MSOs), 13
medical staff
cultural assessment tool, 62–63
roles and responsibilities, 22
traditional integration models, 21–22
Medicare, *see also* Centers for Medicare and
Medicaid Services (CMS)
accountable care organizations, 82
cardiology alignment, 17
demographics impact, 122
historical developments, 6
as mandatory entitlement program, 10
physicians and specialists, 68
reimbursement percentage, 43
Medicare Payment Advisory Commission
(MedPAC), 71
mergers, stability, 62
messenger model, 36–37
Methodist Le Bonheur Healthcare (MLH),
105–106
metrics
comparison, 50–52
full integration, 123–124

mission work, 49
misuse, integration models, 74
MLH, *see* Methodist Le Bonheur Healthcare (MLH)
models
    accountable care organizations, 80–81
    alignment models, 41–42
    bundled payments, 15
    call coverage, 25–27
    clinical integration, 68–69
    foundation model, 56
    full integration, 121–122
    healthcare costs, shared savings, 90, 91
    hospitals workshop, 6
    medical directorships, 23–25
    medical staff, 21–22
    types, 13–14
    vs. complexity chart, 16
MSO, *see* Medical service organizations (MSOs)
Myers, Nancy A., 112–115

N

National Committee for Quality Assurance (NCQA), 82, 88
national projection expenditures, 8, 9
negative incentives, 15
New England Journal of Medicine, 10
new physician hires, 51
noncompete covenant, 49
nontrauma centers, 25
Norton Healthcare System, 110–112

O

"occurrence policy," 50
office-based physicians, 7
Office of the Inspector General (OIG)
    legal limitations, integration, 74
    medical directorships, 23
on-call coverage and payment
    integration model, 14
    traditional integration models, 25–27
operational support, 47
orthopedics, 33
outcomes, 18
outpatient follow-up, 68
outside activities, 49
oversight board, *see* Governance
overuse, integration models, 74
ownership *vs.* integration, 16

P

patient advocacy representatives, 58
patient-centered focus, 83
patient-centered medical home (PCMH)
    accreditation, 88
    concepts, 80, 89–90
    defined, 86, 88
    demonstration project, 88
    financial studies, 88, 90
    healthcare costs, shared savings model, 90, 91
    home as hub, 88, 91
    information technology infrastructure, 88
    medical neighborhood, 93, 94
    overview, *x,* 86
    payment, joint principles, 92
    physician hospital organization, 38
    startup cost, 81
    Summa Health Systems, 114–115
patient engagement
    accountable care organizations, 84
    full integration, 126–127
Patient Protection and Affordable Care Act (PPACA), *xi*
Patient Referral Act, 72, *see also* Stark Law
payer mix
    current healthcare system, 8–9
    on-call expenditures, 25
payer needs and expectations, 101–102
payer representative, 58
pay-for-performance programs, 59
payments and payment models, *see also* Bundled payments; Compensation
    accountable care organizations, 82, 83
    alignment strategy, 98
    basis for, 14–15
    clinical integration, 74–75
    historical developments, 7
    misalignment of, 41
    on-call expenditures, 14, 25, 27
    patient-centered medical home, 92
    physician employment, 49, 59–61
    reforms, 71
    third-party payment structure, 8
PCMH, *see* Patient-centered medical home (PCMH)
penicillin discovery, 5
per capita expenditure
    age comparisons, 9–10
    country comparisons, 1–2
    healthcare projections, 10–11

percentage Medicare reimbursement, 43
Performance Alliance, 26
performance-based system, 121–122
pharmaceutical advertising, 6
PHO, *see* Physician hospital organization (PHO)
physician alignment strategy, 97–98
physician employment, *see* Employment
physician hospital organization (PHO)
    allowed activities, 36–37
    governance, 57
    overview, 35–38
physicians
    adding value to hospital system, 24
    agreements, 48–50
    cultural assessment tool, 62–63
    engaging framework, 23
    and hospital trust, 17–18
    leadership, 125–126
    on-call expenditures, 25, 27
    readiness, 100
    younger *vs.* older, viewpoints, 25, 27
physician service agreements (PSAs), 56–57
Piedmont Healthcare, 109–110
political sustainability, 35
population health, 84, 124–125
PPO, *see* Preferred provider organization (PPO)
    networks
PPS, *see* Prospective payment system (PPS)
practice, *see* Private practice
preferred provider organization (PPO) networks,
    36
prepaid insurance plans, 5
preventive care, 15
Pricewaterhouse Coopers (PWC) survey, 17
primary care physician, lack of, 68
primary care shortage, 101
private practice
    acquisition purchases, 52
    appraisal, 51
    current environment, 43
    size, office-based physicians, 7
    valuation, 44
    vs. selling to hospital system, 51, 53–55
professional service agreements (PSAs), 56–57
profit sharing, 30
progress *vs.* change, 128
pros, *see* Advantages and benefits
prospective payment system (PPS), 6
ProvenCare program, 108
proxy relative value unit (RVU), 60–61
PSA, *see* Physician service agreements (PSAs)
PWC, *see* Pricewaterhouse Coopers (PWC) survey

Q

quality initiatives, 63
quality scores, 59–60
questions for self, 51

R

RBRVS, *see* Resource-Based Relative Value Scale
    (RBRVS)
readiness, physician, 100
readmissions
    clinical integration, 68–69
    payment incentive basis, 15
referrals
    employment agreement, 48
    patterns, 16
regional health information organizations
    (RHIOs), 68
relationships, stability, 62
relative value unit (RVU)
    payment models, 59–61
    physician service agreements, 56
Resource-Based Relative Value Scale (RBRVS), 6
resources, hospital employment, 51
revenue activities, 49
RHIO, *see* Regional health information
    organizations (RHIOs)
risk
    accountable care organizations, 85
    physician hospital organization, 36
Rogers, Will, 128
roles and responsibilities
    medical directorships, 24–25
    medical staff, 22
    providers, 14
RVU, *see* Relative value unit (RVU)

S

Sacks, Lee, 67
"safe harbor" of employment, 43
Sams, James, 109–110
satisfaction scores, 60
savings opportunities, 86
services and service lines, 30–33
shared savings model, healthcare costs, 90, 91
shifting costs, 8, 10
shift in treatment, 85
sign-on bonuses, 49
"silver tsunami," 8
Social Security Act, 5, 10

speaking engagements, 49
specialists as primary care physician, 68
specialties, employment by, 45–46, 51
special work needs, 49
stability, 62
staff
    alignment strategy, 98–99
    cultural assessment tool, 62
    hospital employment considerations, 51
Stark Law
    clinical co-management, 30
    legal limitations, integration, 72
    medical directorships, 24
Steel, Glenn J, Jr., 107
Stern, David, *ix–x*
stipends, 42
strategic alignment, 47
strategic fit, 35
structure, co-management, 30–32
subsidiaries, 48
success factors, 37–38
Sullivan Cotter, 27
Summa Health Systems, 112–115
surveys
    full integration, 126
    on-call arrangements, 27
    on-call coverage, 26
    Pricewaterhouse Coopers survey, 17
systems strategic alignment initiatives
    Baylor Health Care System, 115–117
    Geisinger Health System, 106–108
    hospital physician integration, 115–117
    Methodist Le Bonheur, 105–106
    Norton Healthcare System, 110–112
    Piedmont Healthcare, 109–110
    Summa Health Systems, 112–115

T

tail coverage, 50
technology developments, 84

telemedicine, 84
third-party payment structure, 8
tipping point, 43
traditional integration models
    call coverage, 25–27
    medical directorships, 23–25
    medical staff, 21–22
training
    Baylor Health Care System, 115–117
    vs. future developments, *ix–x*
transformation, 127–128
transparency
    employment issues, 44
    full integration, 123–124
    governance, 58
trauma centers, 25
treatment shift, 85
trends, insurance, 10
trust, 35

U

underuse, integration models, 74
United States, 8, 9
Utilization Review Accreditation Committee
        (URAC), 88

V

valuation, private practice, 44
values, shared, 47
variable payment models, 59
volume, payment models, 15, 59

W

welfare system, 5
Wolter, Nick, 74
work/life balance, 27
World War II, 5
writing books, 49